T0286369

HOW TO
CLEAR YOUR HOME OF
GHOSTS & SPIRITS

About the Author

Debi Chestnut has been able to see and speak to ghosts her whole life. A paranormal researcher for more than thirty years, she gives lectures and conducts workshops to help people better understand paranormal activity. Debi lives in Michigan with her husband, three black cats, and two dogs.

Visit her online at www.myparanormaladvisor.com.

DEBI CHESTNUT

Tips & Techniques
from a Professional
Ghost Hunter

HOW TO
CLEAR YOUR HOME OF
GHOSTS
& SPIRITS

Llewellyn Publications
Woodbury, Minnesota

FIRST EDITION
Fourth Printing, 2023

Cover art: iStockphoto.com/12295389/diane39
Cover design by Ellen Lawson

Llewellyn Publications is a registered trademark of Llewellyn Worldwide Ltd.

Library of Congress Cataloging-in-Publication Data
Chestnut, Debi.
  How to clear your home of ghosts & spirits : tips & techniques from a professional ghost hunter / Debi Chestnut. — First edition.
      pages   cm
   ISBN 978-0-7387-3931-1
1. Ghosts. 2. Haunted houses 3. Spirits. 4. Parapsychology. 5. Occultism. I. Title. II. Title: How to clear your home of ghosts and spirits.
   BF1461.C48 2014
   133.1—dc23
                            2013042072

Llewellyn Worldwide Ltd. does not participate in, endorse, or have any authority or responsibility concerning private business transactions between our authors and the public.
  All mail addressed to the author is forwarded, but the publisher cannot, unless specifically instructed by the author, give out an address or phone number.
  Any Internet references contained in this work are current at publication time, but the publisher cannot guarantee that a specific location will continue to be maintained. Please refer to the publisher's website for links to authors' websites and other sources.

Llewellyn Publications
A Division of Llewellyn Worldwide Ltd.
2143 Wooddale Drive
Woodbury, MN 55125-2989
www.llewellyn.com

Printed in the United States of America

Other books by Debi Chestnut

Is Your House Haunted?: Poltergeists, Ghosts or Bad Wiring

Contents

INTRODUCTION

One of the first questions I get as a paranormal investigator is "How do I get rid of the ghost in my house?" Unfortunately, there's no simple answer to that question.

The truth is, how you get rid of a ghost depends largely upon what type of ghost you have. There are many different types of ghosts, each with their own set of characteristics and temperaments. (More about different types of ghosts will be explained in greater detail in later chapters.)

For example, the way you get rid of a good spirit is different from how you handle a spirit who is showing malice or is being mischievous. When it comes to ghosts and spirits, knowledge is power and fear is the enemy.

Society and the media, through books and movies, have conditioned us to be afraid of ghosts, when in reality most ghosts mean no harm and there's no reason to fear them. The important thing to remember when it comes to ghosts is that you have to become empowered and claim your home, not give away your power to fear. The goal of this book is to empower you by giving you the knowledge you need to deal with the ghost that has taken up residence in your home. Here are some things to keep in mind while reading:

- Not all ghosts are bad, but they can startle and scare people, which is totally understandable. The main thing you need to remember is that most ghosts are just like us. They were once alive, and are still alive in some way, just without a body. Many ghosts don't mean to scare us; they are simply looking for a way to communicate or make contact with us. So unless you or someone in your family is being physically harmed by a ghost, there really is nothing to fear.

- This book will help you identify the type of ghost or spirit you have and the proper method to get rid of it. Trying to clear your home of a ghost using the wrong method could cause more harm than good, as it could only make the ghost angry and escalate its behavior.

- Keep in mind that sometimes these methods don't work for various reasons. The main reason is that the person using the method doesn't believe it's going to work. It's very important that you believe fully that what you are doing will accomplish your goal.

- In addition, some ways to get rid of a ghost only will work on a negative spirit and not on a ghost with good-will. In some ways, friendly ghosts are more difficult to get rid of because their intent is not to cause harm. In many cases, they just want to be around the living, and convincing that type of ghost to leave can be challenging, but there are techniques you can use.

There are also particular ghosts you shouldn't even try to get rid of yourself, but instead call a paranormal investigator to determine the safest way to make the ghost leave. This book will give you the tools you need to select a reputable paranormal investigator to assist you.

When it comes to ridding a home or other location of a ghost, it may be necessary to repeat the techniques in this book more than once. It's rare that a ghost will leave after your first attempt. They may quiet down for a while, but it might also be necessary to repeat the method several times before your home is completely clean and ghost-free.

I've been a paranormal investigator for well over twenty years and have been witness to what most of the types of ghosts outlined in this book can do. I've seen the effects that ghosts can have on people's lives and on my own life—both good and bad.

I'm also a medium/sensitive and have been able to see and communicate with ghosts and spirits for as long as I can remember, so it's only natural that I would end up being a paranormal investigator.

While some people who have gifts have chosen to ignore them, I've made the choice to embrace my gifts and use them to help as many people as I possibly can. One of the main ways I reach lots of people and assist them with their paranormal issues is through my books.

I also work with Black River Paranormal, a ghost-hunting team of dedicated and knowledgeable paranormal investigators. We work hard to help people understand and deal with any paranormal activity going on in their homes, places of business, and places of worship.

To make this book easy to follow and understand, I've divided the different types of ghosts into categories based on whether they are active, angry, benign, and so on. Some types of ghosts and spirits belong in more than one classification, and I've included that information where appropriate in the ghost's individual definitions.

I believe that ghosts in general are greatly misunderstood by most people, and if this book assists you in not only understanding why some ghosts do what they do but also helps you clear your house of ghosts, then I've accomplished my goal.

Just to clarify, ghosts and spirits are, according to many paranormal researchers, different. Ghosts are people who have died but have not crossed over to the other side, while spirits are people who have died, crossed over to the other side, and then decided for whatever reason to come back to the earthly plane.

If you are unsure about what type of ghost or spirit occupies your home, have any questions, or need more advice, you are always free to contact me at debichestnut@yahoo.com.

Happy Hauntings!

Debi Chestnut

CHAPTER ONE

IS IT REALLY A GHOST?

In my twenty-plus years of paranormal investigating, it's been my experience that many times when people believe they have a ghost or spirit, there really is a logical explanation for what's happening in their home or workplace. In my book *Is Your House Haunted?* I cover this topic in great detail, but for purposes of this book, we're just going to touch on the subject, and I'm going to give you a crash course in possible causes for what appears to be paranormal activity. Just because you believe something paranormal is happening, don't let it scare you. Step back, take a couple of deep breaths, and first try to determine if there's a logical, non-ghostly explanation for it.

TIME TO CALL AN ELECTRICIAN?

What seems like ghostly activity can commonly be attributed instead to electrical issues. If you're experiencing lights going on and off by themselves, call in a licensed electrician to check for any possible electrical issues—and, if any are found, have them repaired. If after any repairs you're still experiencing the same issues, then it's possible you have an unwanted guest in the form of a ghost or spirit in your home.

HIGH ELECTROMAGNETIC FIELDS (EMFs)

While the electrician is there, have him or her use an EMF detector to pick up any possible high electromagnetic fields in your home or place of business.

In the paranormal world, we call a high electromagnetic field a *fear cage*. This is because high electromagnetic fields can cause hallucinations, the feeling that you're being watched, and/or tingling throughout your body, as well as other symptoms depending on the person. People's bodies can react differently to high EMFs, but the symptoms above are the most common ones that seem to manifest in most people.

All of the above symptoms can be attributed to having a ghost or other type of phantom in your home, but before you jump to conclusions, have an electrician check out the EMF readings in your home or workplace.

I recently dealt with a case where the people reported tingling in their legs, the feeling that they were being watched, and the sensation of being attacked in their sleep. Even I was pretty convinced they had a demonic entity on their hands.

The Catholic Church came in more than once and performed house blessings and mild exorcisms of the property in an attempt to get rid of what was there, but to no avail.

The people living in this house finally called an electrician, who discovered that their electrical boxes weren't grounded and high EMFs were present all over the house. Once everything was fixed properly, all the feelings and experiences stopped immediately.

DID IT JUST GET COLD IN HERE?

There's a theory among paranormal investigators that cold spots in a location could be attributed to the presence of a ghost or spirit. The theory is that in order to manifest, a ghost needs energy. The ghost, or other type of entity, will suck all the energy out of a room like a giant vacuum, causing the room to become cold; in extreme cases, a room can become so cold that you'll be able to see your breath.

The non-paranormal explanation for this would be that there's a draft coming from an open or leaky window or door, or that there's something wrong with the heating system in the location.

Check for drafts around windows and doors, and call in a licensed heating and cooling specialist to check out the furnace and the complete heating system, including any ductwork, to ensure that everything is running as it should.

THERE'S A PROBLEM WITH THE DOORS

Another frequent complaint among people who believe their house is haunted is the fact that doors and cabinets seem to open and/or close by themselves. While this type of activity can be attributed to the presence of a ghost or spirit, more than likely the doors themselves need to be adjusted.

Check the hinges on the doors or cabinets and see that they are properly adjusted or if they need to be replaced. Try shutting the doors and walking around the room especially close to the doors, and see if that causes them to open. Also check the latches on the doors or cabinets and make sure they are closing and latching properly. Another thing you may want to check is if there are any drafts inside or outside the room that could cause the doors or cabinets to open or close by themselves.

Doors or cabinets opening by themselves can also be due to forgetfulness either by yourself or someone in your household; it can even be caused by your pets.

I personally have had this happen. I knew there was a shadow person in my home because I'd seen him, and I would go upstairs to the bathroom and find one or more of the drawers in the vanity open. Of course, I attributed this to the shadow man. Then one day I tried to shut the drawer and hit something solid. Just then one of my cats popped her head out from behind the drawer and crawled over the back of the drawer, over the top of the drawer, and casually sauntered out of the bathroom to find another suitable place to sleep—problem solved.

FOOTSTEPS

Many people who believe their house is haunted report hearing footsteps. Sometimes these footsteps are random, but in other cases the footsteps seem to occur at the same time of day or night on a rather regular basis.

In many instances, this is caused by a residual haunting (see chapter 3), but it could also be caused by a house settling; by plumbing issues, such as water running through the pipes or the pipes expanding and contracting due to temperature changes; by the heat vents expanding or contracting; or by other non-ghostly situations. The sound of footsteps can also be explained by loose pipes banging against a floor joist as water runs through them.

Make sure all pipes are securely attached to the joists and that they aren't banging around and causing these noises.

COULD THERE BE CRITTERS IN THE WALLS?

I've talked to lots of people who believe their house is haunted, and in many cases they report hearing scratching noises in the walls and/or attic areas of their homes.

The first thing I tell them to do is to have a pest-removal company come to their home or workplace and check for small animals—such as mice, rats, squirrels, and bats—that may have gotten into their space.

I also have them check out their chimneys for small animals that may have gotten trapped there. In addition, I tell them to check for tree branches or a loose gutter that may be scraping the roof or outside walls of their home and to remove these branches or the loose gutter.

In most cases the above remedies seem to solve the problem; however, if you check these things and still are hearing the scratching noises, then you could have a ghost or spirit occupying your home or business.

I had a family who was frantic call me in to investigate scratching noises coming from their family room; they were terrified. Upon closer inspection of the family room and after interviewing the family, I believe I knew what the problem was. After retrieving a powerful flashlight from my car, I scampered to the second floor of their home and crawled out the bathroom window onto the roof of their family room. I made my way across the roof to the chimney and used my flashlight to inspect the inside of the chimney. Sure enough, a family of raccoons was trapped on the flue shelf.

The family immediately called in a critter-removal service, and the raccoons were safely removed and transported to a wooded area and released back into the wild.

Now, I know you're asking, "How did you know?" The answer is really quite simple: I had the same thing happen in my own home—experience is a great teacher.

SHADOWS AND STRANGE LIGHTS

There may be times when you catch a shadow or some kind of strange-looking light out of the corner of your eye, or see it move or flash against a wall in your home or business. This activity could lead some people to believe that their house is haunted by a ghost, spirit, or other type of entity, such as a shadow person.

If this happens to you, make sure no one has walked outside by a window or door, or someone in your house didn't just simply walk by and the light caused their shadow to appear on a wall. Also make sure a car didn't go down the street causing the event, especially if it's at night.

I understand that most of us are used to what a car going down the street at night looks like in our home, but sometimes you're really not sure, so double-check these things before you jump to the conclusion that a ghostly presence has invaded your home.

This kind of thing happened to me once, and it just about drove me crazy trying to figure it out. Here's what happened: I was sitting at my computer, writing, and in the reflection of my computer screen I noticed a shadow passing back and forth behind me, yet I couldn't ascertain if it was in the same room, or where it was coming from. It didn't look like a human shadow but more of a misshapen black mist. Every time I turned around, nothing was there.

I kept typing so that whatever was there would think I was ignoring it, and the shadow kept passing behind me for a few more seconds before vanishing completely. I got up and walked around the room, trying to pick up the presence of a ghost or spirit, or at the very least the residual energy of a presence—but I couldn't feel a thing.

Frustrated, I sat back down and continued writing for quite some time with no further incident, until it showed up again. This time I leapt from my chair and whirled around expecting to confront a spirit, but instead noticed that I'd left the window blind completely up and the neighbor across the boat canal from us had their back light on. I then noticed one of my black cats sitting on the back of the couch staring at me like I'd lost what little was left of my mind.

I walked back over to my desk and peered at the computer screen, which sits up rather high on a shelf on my desk. Sure enough, the light was refracting on my window at just the right angle so that every time the cat walked back and forth looking for bugs on the window, an eerie, indistinguishable black shadow would appear on my screen. Mystery solved. I shut the blind and had no further incidents. So, yes, even a skilled paranormal investigator can be mistakenly led to believe there's some kind of phantom in their presence, when in reality it's just a curious cat looking for bugs.

WIRELESS DEVICES

I know it sounds strange, but devices such as garage door openers and remote-control ceiling fans can make you think you have a mischievous ghost if you don't know what to look for. The only reason I know this is because I had a situation arise in my own home that pretty much made me insane until I figured it out.

The ceiling fan in my breakfast room would go on and off by itself and change speeds, and the light would go from bright to dim and back again by itself. I thought for sure I had a poltergeist.

One day my neighbor and I were talking, and she said that her garage door would go up and down by itself for no apparent reason. After a little experimentation, we figured it out.

My husband had installed a remote control for the ceiling fan in the breakfast room, and it was on an outside wall right by our neighbor's garage wall. Anyway, the ceiling fan transmitter and her garage door opener were on the same frequency.

Every time she opened or closed her garage door, my ceiling fan would do something stupid. In addition, every time I used the remote control to adjust the ceiling fan, it would open or shut her garage door. After changing the frequency on the ceiling-fan transmitter, all the bizarre activity stopped.

So if you're experiencing the same type of activity and are married to and/or live next door to a gadget freak, you may want to compare frequencies on the transmitters to see if that stops what appears to be any paranormal activity.

× × ×

As you can plainly see, there are lots of logical reasons for perceived paranormal activity, and the list only covers the most common types of purported ghostly activity.

It's very important that you don't jump to the conclusion that you have a ghost, but rather look for a logical explanation for any bizarre or unusual events that you may encounter. True hauntings are extremely rare, and demonic or other hauntings by an inhuman are rarer still.

So if after looking for a common cause to an extraordinary event, you can't find one, then you can attempt to get rid of your unwanted houseguest yourself by following the guidelines in this book, or you can call in a paranormal investigator to assist you and to help you determine if there is a ghost present, or if there's an explanation you hadn't thought of that could be causing the activity.

CHAPTER TWO

LET'S TALK ABOUT GHOSTS

The word *ghost* conjures up different images to many people. Hollywood has been gracious enough to introduce us to a wide variety of ghosts, spirits, demons, and other ghoulish creatures throughout cinematic history.

The truth of the matter is most real ghosts aren't scary at all and simply want to convey a message, be acknowledged, or simply let us know they are there. The problem is, we have been conditioned by the same movies and television shows that teach us about ghosts to be afraid of them.

The real question you should ask yourself is "Do I really want to get rid of the ghost?"

Granted, there are some ghosts the living should fear, but they are few and far between. Generally, ghosts mean no harm, and it's important to remember that the majority of ghosts that walk among us were once human too and still have many of their human characteristics—except, of course, a body.

Most people believe that any type of paranormal activity means their house or place of business is haunted. The truth is a true haunting is very rare, and just because you may be experiencing paranormal activity doesn't mean your house is haunted.

The word *paranormal* means something that defies rational explanation, but most alleged paranormal activity can be attributed to something not out of the ordinary.

If you believe you are experiencing paranormal activity, you may want to read my book *Is Your House Haunted?* in order to determine if you do indeed have a ghost, or if the activity you're experiencing has an earthly explanation.

It is important to remember that there are some types of ghosts you don't need to try to get rid of, because such ghosts will go away when their purpose for remaining here has been fulfilled. Either that or they will simply fade away over time.

My experience with working with different people over the years is that some people become attached to their ghosts, and don't really want to let them go so they can cross over to the "other side."

However, if the ghost is being particularly active and is a nuisance, the different methods contained in this book can be used for that very purpose.

Once you determine that you do indeed have a ghost, then this is the book for you. In this book I will cover various ways that I've found to be successful in ridding your home of an unwanted guest.

Paranormal investigators have put ghosts in specific classifications based on the type of behavior they exhibit. For the purposes of this book, I've classified ghosts as *benign*, *active*, *messengers*, *mysterious*, and so on. This arrangement allows you to go to the specific section most appropriate to your situation.

BENIGN GHOSTS

Benign ghosts are harmless ghosts and spirits that show up once in a while, either at specific times of the year or simply to let you know they are there.

Benign ghosts may or may not make any attempt to interact with the living, and in some cases, no real ghost is present. It's what is referred to as a *residual haunting* and is normally an event from the past caught in a type of time warp that keeps replaying itself over and over, like a tape player on a residual loop.

A benign ghost can show up as a full-body apparition on a battlefield or ship, or in a place of business or your home. Normally, benign ghosts are going about their business the way they did when they were alive.

A benign ghost might be seen opening and closing doors and walking (which can account for footsteps you may hear)—sometimes even walking through walls. There is nothing you can do to get rid of this activity, and generally it will disappear all by itself over time.

In cases such as historical ghosts and apparitions, they can either be *intelligent ghosts*—meaning they will try to interact with you in some way—or *residual energy* that is simply replaying a certain event over and over, like a tape recorder that is looping.

Whichever type of ghost it is, intelligent or residual, there is no way to get rid of them, as they will leave on their own, and other than giving you a good scare, they pose no threat to the living.

Some of the most common benign ghosts are as follows:

Anniversary Ghosts

This type of ghost will appear on the date of an anniversary that held some meaning for them when they were alive. It could be the anniversary of their birth, death, wedding day, or the like. They could also appear on another special occasion, such as the birth of a child.

Anniversary ghosts will always acknowledge you in some way. They may attempt to speak to you, look at you, or cause some type of activity that lets you know they are there and who they are.

If you have a picture of deceased loved ones on display, they could cause that picture to move or fall over to let you know it's them. If you're taking pictures on the day of a special event that was celebrated when your loved ones were alive, invite them to join in—you're never sure who's going to show up in the photograph!

As an example, every year on my birthday, my dad finds a way to tell me happy birthday. He might appear briefly before me, or sometimes I will find an unlit birthday candle placed in the center of my desk. It's just his little way of showing how easy it is for love to transcend death.

If you have an anniversary ghost, it doesn't mean your house is haunted, because this type of ghost will only appear on a specific date or dates each year and not be present at any other time. There is no need to attempt to get rid of this type of ghost because it will leave on its own. It is also possible that an anniversary ghost may only appear one or twice on the important date and then not return at all.

Apparitions

In the world of the paranormal, an *apparition* is defined as any type of a ghostly figure. Apparitions are broken down into four classifications: *partial*, *invisible*, *visible*, and *solid*.

Partial Apparitions

Partial apparitions normally don't have a complete body. They could be missing a head, for example, or instead you might only see the head. There doesn't appear to be any rhyme or reason as to which body part may be missing. In some cases, a person may only see a hand, a set of legs, or the entire upper or lower half of the apparition's body.

Partial apparitions generally are benign and will fade away as quickly as they appear, although I do admit that seeing one can startle a person.

For example, you might walk through a room and see a head floating in the air, or you could see just a pair of legs going up a stairway.

Invisible Apparitions

The term *invisible apparition* might sound like an oxymoron, but it is really defined as a ghost that can't be seen with the naked eye and shows up in a photo or on video.

An invisible apparition may show up as a shadow, or as solid as you and me. It could be standing right next to you, and it's possible you'd never know it—unless you were taking a photo or had a camcorder running in the room at the time it was there.

I had this very thing happen when I was wandering around an allegedly haunted cemetery one day. Armed only with my sixth sense and a digital camera, I trudged through the cemetery on a warm fall day, snapping pictures whenever a stray patch of energy caught my attention. Other than something draining the batteries in my camera—twice—the day seemed relatively uneventful.

When I got home, I slid the SD card out of my camera and into my computer to review the pictures—I was pretty sure I didn't catch anything, but it was worth a look.

I clicked through the pictures, studying each one carefully for any anomaly that might show up. Then I hit a picture that took my breath away. Walking among the tombstones was the apparition of a woman in a long, frontier-style dress and a bonnet. She appeared to be carrying what resembled a basket in her hands.

After recovering from the shock, I enlarged the picture and ran it through some filtering software in an attempt to clear up the image a little bit, but the evidence was there. I clicked through the other pictures, and in the picture taken immediately after the one with the apparition, there was nothing there but tombstones. To date, it's one of my favorite photos.

I've been back to the cemetery numerous times but have been unable to debunk the picture or get the ghostly image of the young woman again.

Visible Apparitions

Visible apparitions generally are seen with the naked eye but can appear to be transparent or semitransparent. In other words, you may be able to see through them.

In some cases, you may be able to make out what clothes these apparitions are wearing and even their physical characteristics. In other cases, the apparition may only appear as a white, cloudy mist. The mist might take the rough shape of a person or not.

For example, you might see a white mist appear in the room you're in and linger for a minute or two and disappear, or the mist could float out of the room into another part of the house.

Sometimes seeing through them is the only way you will be able to tell if they are an apparition or a living person.

Solid Apparitions

Solid apparitions will appear as real as any living person, and you might even acknowledge them as you would anyone else—until they disappear before your very eyes.

For example, you could walk into a restaurant and see someone standing out of the way, or sitting alone at a table, who seems to be a little out of place, but you can't quite put your finger on why. You may turn away for just a split second and that person will be gone. You'll quickly scan the restaurant because you're positive they didn't walk by you, but you won't see them. If this happens, you've probably just experienced a solid apparition.

Solid apparitions are a little tricky for me because I'm able to see ghosts and spirits if they choose to appear before me. About the only way I can tell if a solid apparition is a ghost is if it communicates telepathically with me—if it doesn't, then it's a living person. Strange, I know, but welcome to my world.

Historical Ghosts

There are times when a ghost or multiple ghosts will attach themselves to a location such as a battlefield or another historical location.

Very rarely will historical ghosts interact with the living and go about their activities as they did when they were alive.

Most of the time they will appear in clothing common to the era in which they lived.

There have been many reports throughout the years of ghosts on Civil War battlefields, and paranormal researchers, tourists, and workers regularly report spotting soldiers in Civil War uniforms, the sound of musket fire, and/or cannon fire.

Most of the time, historical ghosts fall into the category known as *residual hauntings*. Because of the violence of a military battle, it wouldn't be unusual for this energy to manifest itself in the form of soldiers still fighting a war, but it doesn't mean that these brave men and women are still here fighting an eternal war. It simply means that because of the trauma of war, the energy will keep playing the event over and over like a video playing in a continuous loop.

For example, there have been many reports of seeing wounded soldiers from people who bought homes that were used as hospitals or morgues during the Civil War.

There's really no way to get rid of historical ghosts, because most of the time they are not ghosts at all but residual energy that may or may not fade away over time. If a historical ghost is not residual energy, then it is tied to the building or the land.

What is the easiest way to tell if a historical ghost is residual energy or an intelligent haunting? If it tries to interact with the world of the living, then you know it's an intelligent haunting.

If the haunting is not residual but an actual ghost, it is perfectly harmless and there's no real need to attempt to get rid of it.

Traveling and/or Hitchhiking Ghosts

Traveling, or *hitchhiking*, ghosts are the types of spirits that spawn urban legends all over the world.

A hitchhiking ghost may only appear on the anniversary of its death, because most of these types of ghosts were killed while hitchhiking and tend to appear at the spot of their death.

This type of spirit will normally appear on one specific road or route and is normally waiting for a train, horse, car, bus, airplane, or some other type of transportation and can appear any time of the day or night.

Resurrection Mary in Chicago is one of the most famous hitchhiking ghost stories around. The urban legend states that Mary was a young woman who was killed on her way home from a dance. Some versions of the story say that she died in front of Resurrection Cemetery. Many people have reported picking up a young female hitchhiker, only to have her disappear when they pass by Resurrection Cemetery.

I have my own hitchhiking ghost. Almost every time I'm driving to or from the house of one of my friends, I smell tobacco coming from the backseat of my car. While I can't see any smoke, the odor is unmistakable—it's cherry tobacco. I only know this because I spent over an hour in a tobacco shop one day, smelling all the different kinds of tobacco until I found the right one.

I first notice the smell when I pass by the cemetery on the way to my friend's house, and then it disappears when I stop at a stop sign in front of a location that used to be the site of a pre–Civil War mansion.

On the way home from my friend's house, I will smell the tobacco at the stop sign, and then it disappears when we pass by the cemetery. This doesn't happen all the time, mind you, but frequently enough to catch my attention.

I've tried several times to communicate with the spirit, but so far no response. He just seems content to sit in the backseat for the short ride to the stop sign. He did finally show himself to me one day. I smelled the smoke and glanced in my rear-view mirror.

I could see that he must have been a very distinguished man in life and quite the gentleman. He is an older man in his late sixties if I had to guess, and he wears the type of very expensive-looking three-piece suit that would have been common in the late nineteenth century.

His hair, mostly gray, is impeccably combed and his moustache neatly waxed and groomed. He appears to be rather portly but, in my opinion, a man of class.

I have to admit that when he does show up, which is less frequently now, I talk to him aloud and tell him about my day and what's going on in my life. I'm positive that the people in passing cars must think I'm nuts, but I don't really care. My hitchhiker listens politely and fades away at the stop sign.

ACTIVE GHOSTS

When most people hear the word *ghost*, they believe it to mean the spirit of a person or animal who is deceased and can appear, using various means, to the living. Sometimes a ghost can appear as a mist, a shadow, or as real as you or me.

Ghosts will normally haunt certain locations, objects, and/or people that were familiar to them when they were alive, and there have been reports of ghostly armies, ships, and animals.

Many different types of ghosts fall under the classification of active ghosts. Poltergeists, avengers, child ghosts, ghosts that haunt, and most types of inhumans such as demons all fall under this category for one simple reason: they all can cause a great amount of paranormal activity.

Traditional or intelligent hauntings are normally the product of an active ghost. These types of spirits are capable of turning on and off lights, opening and closing doors, and rapping, tapping, and knocking on walls, doors, windows, etc. The more malevolent types of active ghosts can push, bite, scratch, and punch living people, sometimes causing serious harm.

Active ghosts will almost always acknowledge and/or interact with the living and their environment in some way to let you know they are present. Most of the time these types of spirits just want to be acknowledged by the living in some way or deliver a message, while some other types of active spirits—such as demons, avengers, and others—

set out to intentionally cause havoc and, in some cases, make the life of the living into a real mess.

Just because you're experiencing paranormal activity doesn't mean your house is haunted. In order for a house to be haunted, it must meet certain criteria: the paranormal activity must be consistent, and the ghost or spirit must be intelligent. By *intelligent* I mean that the ghost must try to interact with the living in some manner.

A prime example is from my own personal experience with an active ghost.

I met Nathaniel when I was the tender age of five. He lived on the second floor of my great-aunt Tote's house, which contained two bedrooms and deep, winding closets that I was convinced held mysterious, wonderful things. Since my great-aunt only occupied the first floor of the house, the second floor was used mainly for storing long-forgotten antiques, books, furniture, and other items generally reserved for an attic. It was the perfect place for a ghost—and a curious child.

My parents were out of town for the weekend, so, as usual, I was left with my great-aunt, a wonderful woman whom I loved as much as life itself. She lay down to take a nap after making me promise I wouldn't leave the house, which left me free to explore the second floor.

I made my way up the steep staircase and turned the corner at the landing to walk down the hallway. On my right was a huge bedroom that held boxes of books, furniture, and scads of other items just begging for me to investigate them.

Sitting cross-legged on the floor, I was eagerly emptying out a box when I felt someone enter the room. I looked up and saw the figure of a man dressed in old-fashioned britches, suspenders, and a billowy white shirt. His dark hair was shaggy and mussed, and his keen eyes darted around the room nervously. He looked like someone out of *Little House on the Prairie*. Yet, something seemed off about this man— something not quite right. I could see through him into the hallway!

"Who are you?" I asked, looking at him with childlike wonder.

"I'm Nathaniel," he answered. Yet he didn't speak the words; they just popped into my head.

"Hi, Nathaniel, are you a ghost?" I said.

"Yes. But please don't be afraid of me. I'm so lonely," Nathaniel pleaded.

"I'm not scared of you," I assured him. "I get kind of lonely too. We can be friends!"

And so began several years of a unique friendship. When I was at my great-aunt's house, I spent countless hours in the attic with Nathaniel. He'd watch me while I colored, played, and explored the treasures hidden in the rooms. We shared secrets, but mostly we kept each other company.

Time marched on, and as I got older my trips to the second floor became less frequent, and eventually my great-aunt died and my dad sold her house. Even though I was no longer able to talk to Nathaniel, I thought about him often throughout the years and missed him horribly.

About two months before I got married, the people who had bought my great-aunt's house called my dad and said they were divorcing, and would he like to buy the house back?

My dad jumped at the chance and then sold it to my husband and me for a paltry sum. I couldn't believe my good fortune! I'd be reunited with Nathaniel. I'd learned so much about ghosts over the years, and I now knew that Nathaniel belonged in the light and that I had to figure out a way to cross him over to the other side. No matter what, I had to help my first best friend and confidant.

What I didn't anticipate was that two other ghosts besides Nathaniel were also in the house. This complicated things a bit because I needed to explain to my husband exactly what I am and what I can do. I'd told him before we were married that I could communicate with spirits; however, experience had taught me that to fully make some people aware of what I do tends to scare them off. As my husband is an engineer, the likelihood of him fully understanding the implications of my being a medium would have been an exercise in futility. In fact, he treated it kind of like a joke and would tease me about my "ghost friends" constantly. I had to deal with a rather active ghost immediately upon moving into the house—which is a story I will discuss later in the book.

I did, however, take the time to go up to the second floor and reacquaint myself with Nathaniel. Just as I did when I was a child, I crept up the stairs to the second floor. As I turned the corner to walk down the stairway, I was immediately engulfed by a white mist and what felt like arms wrapping tightly around my body.

"I'm happy to see you too, Nathaniel," I laughed. "Please let me go so we can talk."

The white mist backed away from me and materialized into the Nathaniel I remembered. It was then that I realized that Nathaniel was mentally disabled. I had a cousin who was born with a mental disability, and I recognized the oversized head, clumsy movements, and other symptoms of that condition. Nathaniel cringed when he realized I knew about his impairment.

"Now that you know, you won't talk to me anymore," he said telepathically with profound resignation.

"That's not true," I said. "When did you die?" I settled myself cross-legged on the floor of the hallway.

"1853, I think," he responded tentatively.

"I don't remember anyone in our family history, with the exception of my cousin, who had your condition. Are you a member of my family?" I asked.

"No. I came to this house a long time ago," Nathaniel answered and drifted off into the bedroom to the right of me.

I got up off the floor and followed him. He moved toward the one tall, narrow window in the room that looked out at the side of the house.

"I used to live over there," Nathaniel said.

"Over where?" I asked, joining him at the window.

"On the corner. They destroyed my house to put up another building. I didn't like it there so I came here because the attic was empty," he answered.

"Where the gas station is?" I said, knowing it was the only building not original to the area at the time Nathaniel would have been alive.

"I guess."

"Nathaniel, this isn't an attic. It's the second floor to a house. This room is a bedroom. Why do you think it's an attic?"

"My family was afraid and ashamed of me because they said I was sick, so when we had company or they didn't want to be bothered with me, they made me go up to the attic so no one would see me," Nathaniel said sadly.

"I'm sorry they did that to you," I said, knowing that what he experienced was customary at the time. "So why haven't you gone into the light and crossed over?"

"Everyone laughed at me and made fun of me when I was alive. It was terrible. I just don't want to go through that anymore. That's why I came here. No one could see me and I wouldn't be laughed at. When you were a little girl, you never made me feel different. I'm happy here, now that you're back," Nathaniel answered.

"I understand, but if you go into the light, you will be healed. No one will laugh at you anymore and you can see your family again," I said.

"I don't want to see my family," he said, his energy filled with anger. "I can't talk to you anymore right now." With that he faded away, and I felt his energy was no longer in the room with me. Disappointed, I made my way back down the stairs to the first floor.

I wish I could have made Nathaniel realize that his disability didn't transcend into death and that he was perfectly healthy, but quite frankly I was pretty sure he wouldn't believe me. Additionally, at the time and today, I'm thankful that my gift affords me the ability to understand what ghosts are telling me in complete sentences and not just in bits and pieces—it makes it a lot easier to help them make the transition from this world to the next.

Days turned into weeks, and weeks into months. I became pregnant and gave birth to my son, and then twenty-two months later to my daughter. Nathaniel, while still everpresent, refused to go into the light, and quite frankly I was too busy with my children to spend a lot of time trying to convince him it was in his own best interest to do so.

As my son got older and learned how to talk, I'd hear him in his bedroom, which is the same room on the second floor that Nathaniel hung out in, talking to someone.

"Who are you talking to?" I asked one night after hearing him having a conversation in his bedroom. I sat down on the edge of my son's bed.

"The man, Mommy. He hides when you come up here because he thinks you're going to be mad," my son told me, his dark brown eyes looking earnestly into mine.

"His name's Nathaniel," I told my son. "I used to play with him when I was a little girl."

"You did?" His eyes grew wide.

"Yes, and I won't be mad. He doesn't have to disappear when I come up here," I assured him.

"Is he a ghost?" my son asked.

"Yes, he is. But he's a good ghost and won't hurt you," I said.

"Like Casper?"

"Yes," I laughed. "Just like Casper. Now go to sleep."

I tucked my son into bed and walked slowly down the stairs to the first floor. I have to admit I was a little shaken and proud that my son inherited my gift and could see spirits and wasn't afraid of them. But I also knew that I would have to start to teach him the difference between a good ghost and a bad ghost.

With a heavy sigh, I sat down on the couch in the living room to think. It's hard enough to be a child without having the added burden of being able to see and talk to the dead. I had to figure out a way to help my child understand the spirit world and accept his gift. Time passed, and my son spoke less and less to Nathaniel, although I never asked him why.

One weekend, my husband decided to hang shelves in my son's room to hold his ever-growing collection of toys and treasures. I told him not to hang the shelves on the wall by the window because that's where Nathaniel liked to stand and gaze out at the place his house used to occupy. My husband ignored my pleas and hung the shelves with molly bolts right next to Nathaniel's window and made my son climb the shelves, much against my protestations, to make sure they were strong and sturdy.

A week later my husband and I took the children camping. Upon arriving home late Sunday afternoon, my son raced up the stairs to his bedroom.

"Mom! Come up here!" he cried.

Hearing the fear in his voice, I ran up the stairs and into his bedroom. There I found that the shelves had been ripped from the wall, molly bolts and all, leaving gaping holes in the drywall. It was apparent that the shelves had been thrown violently across the room, leaving the toys scattered everywhere.

I called my husband upstairs, and he stood open-mouthed, gaping at the destruction.

"I told you not to hang the shelves there," I said, as I started to pick up the toys and pile them in one of the corners of the bedroom.

"Well, yeah, but I never thought…" my husband's sentence trailed off, left unfinished.

"You really made Nathaniel mad, Dad," my son said, trying to hide the smile that played around his mouth.

"I guess I did. We won't make the same mistake this time," my husband answered as he picked the shelves up off the floor and stacked them neatly against a wall far away from the window. I could tell he was trying to hide the shock and fear he felt due to Nathaniel's temper tantrum.

We cleaned up the bedroom, and my husband rehung the shelves on the opposite wall from the window, leaving Nathaniel more than ample space to resume his window gazing. The next weekend my husband patched the holes in the wall by the window and gave the wall a fresh coat of paint, although he insisted I be upstairs with him the entire time in case Nathaniel showed up. I never told my husband, but Nathaniel was standing at the doorway of the bedroom the whole time, keeping a close eye on the repairs to ensure that his coveted place by the window wouldn't be impeded.

A few weeks later my parents took the kids with them to visit relatives who lived up north. They would be gone for a few days, and I decided this was the best time to try, once again, to get Nathaniel to go into the light and cross over to the other side.

I went upstairs to my son's room and sat down on his bed.

"Nathaniel, come talk to me," I said. "I'm not mad about the shelves and you're not in trouble."

Within a few seconds Nathaniel appeared at the doorway and immediately made his way to the window, gazing longingly toward the lot where his house once sat.

"I'm sorry for what I did," he said. "I didn't mean to scare the kids."

"You didn't," I assured him. "But you really need to go into the light, Nathaniel. You don't belong here."

"I told you I don't want to see my family," Nathaniel said, anger rising up in his voice.

"I understand that. I really do. But it's for your own good. Have I ever lied to you, Nathaniel?" I said.

"No."

"Then you know I'm not lying when I tell you that if you go into the light you will be healed. You will be normal, just like everyone else, and no one will make fun of you or be mean to you. You will be happier there," I pleaded.

"I'm scared," he said, turning away from the window to look at me.

From the bottom of my heart I wished I could wrap my arms around him and give him a hug in an attempt to comfort him, but words were the only tool at my disposal.

"I know you are, honey. It's okay to be afraid. Would it be okay if I got a friend or two of mine from the other side to come help you? They can tell you what it's like over there, something I can't do," I said.

"I will talk to them," Nathaniel assented.

"That's all I ask," I told him as I got up from the bed and went to stand beside him at the window. "It will be okay, Nathaniel. I promise."

I went downstairs and lay down on my bed, allowing my mind to clear and calling out to my spirit guides. Within a few moments, I felt a ghostly presence enter the room and, telepathically, I told my guide that I needed help in getting Nathaniel into the light and over to the other side where he belonged.

My guide assented, and assured me that the matter would be handled in a loving and caring manner.

I swear I should have installed a revolving door to the other side in my son's room for the next few days. Spirits were popping in and out so fast, and with such frequency, that it made me dizzy because of all the different energies.

The day before my children came home from their trip with my parents, I went upstairs to see how things were progressing with Nathaniel. I wandered from room to room in search of him, but to no avail. Nathaniel was gone—he'd finally made the transition into the light. The house suddenly felt empty, like a hole had opened up in the energy of the home, and the void I felt in my soul was painful. While I was relieved that Nathaniel went into the light, I desperately missed my friend—but it was for the best.

You'd think the story ends there, but it doesn't. A few years after Nathaniel left, we sold the house and bought another house a mile or so away.

The day of the move, I was the last one in the house and walked around to make sure nothing got left behind. I went upstairs and wandered through the empty room my daughter once occupied, and when I turned around to leave, Nathaniel appeared in the doorway. He was no longer disabled, and he appeared strong and robust.

"Nathaniel!" I said. "What are you doing here?"

"I just came to say goodbye, and to thank you. I'm so happy now that I am where I belong. You have always been my best friend in the world, and I will be there to greet you many years from now when it's your time to cross over."

"You're welcome, my friend," I said, tears welling up in my eyes. "I'm so glad you're happy. I miss you and love you."

"I love you too. I will never be far away," he answered.

Nathaniel's energy faded, and once again I was left alone with my thoughts and emotions. While it's not unusual for a spirit to be able to move back and forth between the earthly plane and the other side, I found it particularly comforting to know that Nathanial wanted to come back, even if it was for such a brief period of time.

I took one last look around and walked out of the house, closing the door on that chapter of my life.

An active ghost makes its presence known in many different ways. If you have an active ghost or spirit in your home or business, you'll be acutely aware of its presence.

Avengers

Also known as *revengers*, this type of spirit returns for one of two reasons: either to get revenge against someone living who they believed wronged them in some way when they were alive, or to avenge their death.

For example, a victim of an unsolved murder might keep coming back in an attempt to reveal who killed them. Basically, avenging spirits seek what they perceive to be some kind of justice.

Remember the movie *Ghost*? In the movie, the character played by Patrick Swayze would be classified as an avenger type of spirit because he was seeking justice for his death and wouldn't rest until the person responsible for his death was held accountable. In the meantime, one of his main objectives was to make the life of his killer a living hell.

This type of ghost could appear at the scene of the crime, at its gravesite, or to loved ones in order to seek their help, and this type of ghost will often appear in the clothes it wore when alive.

Spirits out for revenge can be male or female, and many times they appear as apparitions but can't verbalize their needs to the living, but will attempt to communicate in other ways.

They can cause cold spots in rooms or a very sudden drop in temperature. Sometimes the behavior of avenging spirits will be violent toward the person or persons they believe wronged them when they were alive, and they are more than capable of throwing objects, slamming doors, and shoving people down the stairs or in front of cars.

Avengers could continue to appear in the spot of their death or to loved ones still alive for many years and then disappear once they feel justice has been done. In some extreme cases, avengers can harm the living and generally target the living person or persons who wronged them. In other words, as I mentioned, avenging spirits are out to make the life of the person who wronged them a living hell.

Some paranormal investigators and others mistake avenging spirits for demons or poltergeists because of their violent behavior. However, a ghost out for revenge has only one goal: to make life as miserable and terrifying as possible for the person it is targeting until whatever it perceives as justice is served.

I've never personally run into an avenging ghost or spirit, and it's not an experience I would relish. Avenging ghosts or spirits can be one of the most difficult types of entities to get rid of, because they are hell-bent on revenge and / or justice. It would require a great amount of research and experimentation not only to identify who the ghost was when it was alive, but also to convince it that it needs to let go and cross over before its objectives are met.

If you have this type of ghost or spirit in your home or business, you'd be best served by calling in a qualified paranormal investigator or medium to assist you in getting rid of it. The chances of success in making this type of spirit leave before it has extracted its revenge are slim, so you should be prepared to dig in and conduct extensive research to find out the identity of your avenging ghost in order to help it meet its main purpose for being there and finally cross over to the other side. A paranormal investigator worth their salt or a very determined medium should be able to help you achieve this goal.

Child Ghosts

Spirits of children are generally heartbreaking to encounter, although there are exceptions. They are normally lost, scared, and alone. In most cases they are just looking for their mother or father. Their plaintive voices, which might show up during an EVP (electronic voice phenomena) session, calling out to their mothers or fathers, will break your heart.

Other child ghosts may appear to their grieving parents in order to assure them that they are okay and to bring them comfort. There are times, however, when the parents who have suffered the death of a child can't bear to let the child go, and their child is not able to cross over to the other side.

When this type of situation arises, it is heart-wrenching for both the parents and for the child, who is simply waiting for the parents to say it's okay to go and cross over to the other side.

I can't impress on you enough how important it is for parents of a child who is dying or has recently passed away to give that child permission to cross over to the other side; otherwise, the child may be destined to wander the earth as a spirit for eternity—a fate no parent consciously wants for their son or daughter.

On the flip side, there are child ghosts who are perfectly happy residing in a home alongside the living. I've personally run into one of these delightful child spirits. She lives in a house with a couple who were unable to have children.

They are well aware of her presence, and they take great delight in scouring antique stores and flea markets looking for toys that would be familiar to her. They've even converted a spare bedroom into a little girl's room with Victorian furniture, because when the child does appear, she is dressed in a Victorian-era dress. This child ghost is very polite, well mannered, and interactive. She loves bouncing balls down the stairs and having them thrown back up to her. She also enjoys playing with her toys, and the couple has set boundaries as you would with any child.

The couple has conducted extensive research into their home and into all the former owners back to the early 1800s when the house was constructed, but can find no record of a child dying in that home.

In this particular situation, it's very possible that the child ghost resided in a home nearby that at some point was torn down or destroyed, and simply moved into a house she recognized as being there when she was alive.

She was fortunate enough to find a couple who adore her. A very lucky child ghost indeed!

This type of situation is very rare, and personally I'm still struggling with the fact that as happy as this child is, she should eventually cross over to the other side, where she's meant to be. However, that's not my call to make—it's up to the couple who own the house and to the child herself.

Not every haunting by a child ghost turns out as sweetly as in the previous example, however. Sometimes child ghosts can turn mean, vindictive, and bratty. It's my personal belief that they act out in an inappropriate manner because they are scared, alone, and desperate. This doesn't, however, excuse the behavior of some of these child ghosts or spirits.

Child ghosts could become so desperate for company that they may want a living child to join them on a more permanent basis. Although extremely rare, this could lead them to try to kill the living child in order to satisfy their selfish need for companionship.

A child ghost could push a living child out a window or in front of a moving car, or persuade the living child to partake in a harmful activity that may lead to that child's death—all because the child ghost wants company.

I heard about a case a few years ago in which a child ghost who'd been a drowning victim tried to coax a living child to the pond where the ghost, as a child, had drowned many years before. Thankfully, the living child resisted and told his parents, who were, understandably, alarmed. The parents then contacted a paranormal group, who eventually ended up helping this child's poor soul cross over.

As scary as the above scenario sounds, you have to remember we're dealing with a child's mentality, and while they may coerce a living child into these types of activities, child ghosts, in most cases, are not being malicious—just, in a child's mind, seeking friendship and someone to play with.

A child ghost may play with your living child, just as the ghost played when it was alive. This doesn't mean that this ghost is going to try to get your child to join them in death, but it would be wise to keep an eye on the situation and pay special attention when your child mentions what you perceive to be an imaginary friend.

A seemingly violent ghost who throws things, slams doors, and so on could just be a child ghost having a temper tantrum, or it could be something far more dangerous, such as a poltergeist or demon. The most important thing to do is try to determine whether your ghost is a child or another form of spirit.

This can be rather tricky to determine in some situations, and if you're not sure your unseen resident is a child ghost or something else, you may want to call in a paranormal investigator to help you make that determination.

In some cases, a demon can appear as a child spirit in an attempt to make you let your guard down and trust the demon. They do this to gain control over your household. A qualified paranormal investigator should be able to determine if this is the case in your home or business.

Haunting Ghosts

True hauntings, as I've stated before, are very rare, but when they do occur, they may be attributed to a ghost that haunts, or other types of ghosts that will be discussed in this and other chapters.

Haunting ghosts can normally be found in places they loved when they were alive, or around people and/or places they just can't bear to say goodbye to now that they are dead.

Often mistaken for residual hauntings, ghosts that haunt may or may not choose to interact with the living, but just want to linger in a place that made them happy when they were alive. In some cases a haunting ghost could be at a particular location to protect the people living or working there.

Haunting ghosts can be male or female, and will often appear in the same clothes they wore when they were alive. However, they can appear to be human or inhuman at will, and normally haunt only one location.

There is a specific pattern in the behavior of a ghost that haunts, and the living may feel a real sense that a personality is there and that the ghost can think, respond, and communicate with the living who are present in that location—and in many cases such ghosts can.

Haunting ghosts might walk up and down stairs, open or close doors, appear in the room you're in, or exhibit other types of behavior. In many cases a ghost that haunts can be mistaken for other types of ghosts, such as poltergeists. Haunting ghosts may appear many times or choose only to appear once.

As an example, a previous owner of your home may have loved the home so much they don't want to leave. In some cases, the previous owner may not know they're dead and cause a ruckus, but in many cases, they just want to stay in the home they loved so much in life.

Haunting ghosts can also be attached to a person they loved who is still alive—for example, a spouse, best friend, sister, or brother. This does not mean that these spirits are going to possess you—quite the contrary. They just want to be around someone they adored so much in life.

It's possible that these ghosts will give you clues as to who they are, such as moving, knocking over, or manipulating pictures of themselves. They might also do the same thing with mementos that remind you of them or belonged to them when they were alive, such as a piece of favorite jewelry. The piece of jewelry could show up in a conspicuous place, such as on the floor in front of you or on your dresser or kitchen counter—just about anywhere.

When this type of phenomenon occurs, it's just your loved one's way of saying they are there and around you. Knowing who your haunting ghost is should bring you comfort, not frighten you.

Poltergeists

In German, the word *poltergeist* literally means "noisy ghost." This is a name quite befitting this type of ghost, because if you have a poltergeist in your house, there will be noise... and lots of it.

Poltergeists are one of the only types of ghosts that can have a dramatic effect on the world of the living, and they do. They are very skilled at banging on walls and doors, opening and closing cabinets, playing music, making the noise of footsteps, turning lights on and off, flushing toilets, and throwing objects around the room with violent force. They can also change television stations, disconnect telephone calls, and basically manipulate almost anything at their will.

There have been reports of poltergeists pulling hair, tugging on clothes, and pulling bedding off people, and the most malevolent poltergeists can even push, slap, and scratch living people.

These tricksters are more than capable of moving or throwing just about anything, and they can make things disappear and then reappear somewhere else whenever they choose. Poltergeists can also break glass objects and seem to be fond of throwing plates and glasses. In some cases they can ruin clothes and throw rocks, dirt, and stones.

In extreme cases poltergeists have been known to cause the noise of explosions, screams, or voices and make beds violently shake. They can also make water puddles appear out of nowhere, ring telephones and doorbells, and cause physical injury. Simply put, a lot of poltergeists are not friendly ghosts and can make your life a living hell. They could also be classified as ghosts that harm.

Normally poltergeists make little to no attempt to communicate with living people and show no real attachment to the places they choose to haunt. This makes them one of the most difficult types of ghosts to get rid of, because it's next to impossible to determine what they want, if anything.

Poltergeists can also disappear as quickly as they appear. There's simply no rhyme or reason for why they haunt one location, their behavior, or their sudden departure—if they choose to leave.

It's not uncommon for a poltergeist to focus its attention on one particular person in the household, and you may notice an increase in poltergeist activity whenever the target, or *agent*, which is the common term, is around the house.

There's a theory among some paranormal researchers that a lot of poltergeist activity can be attributed to having a teenager in the home. The theory is that because of the rapid changes and raging hormones in a teenager's body, teenagers are, quite by accident, manifesting poltergeist-like activity.

If you have teenagers in your home, pay special attention to who is present when poltergeist activity occurs. If it tends to happen around your teenager or when your teenager is in the same room as the activity, there's a chance that your teen is unconsciously causing these events to happen.

If this is the case, don't get angry with your teenager or tell them to stop it. It's really not their fault, and they aren't even aware they are the cause of the activity. You don't want to lay a huge guilt trip on your child for something that is beyond their control. Just rest assured that once your kid matures physically a little bit more, all the activity will probably stop.

You may also want to pay attention to the stress and anxiety level of your teenager, as this can unconsciously trigger poltergeist-like activity. If you believe your teenager is stressed out or suffering from anxiety, you should discuss this with your family doctor.

Some poltergeists are classified as demons by certain paranormal researchers because they can be so violent and mean. It all depends on the personality of the poltergeist. Some of them can be very mild-mannered and take delight in pulling pranks such as hiding car keys, turning lights on and off, and knocking on doors or walls. The more vindictive poltergeist can make your house look like it's been ransacked.

When dealing with a poltergeist, the most important thing to remember is to speak to them in a firm but calm voice. Don't yell, scream, or threaten a poltergeist because it could do nothing except make the paranormal activity in your house intensify. Your goal is to let them know, without question, that you are the one in control of your house, not them. Even then it may not cause the activity to stop or make the poltergeist leave.

A prime example of this occurred when I worked on a poltergeist case many years ago. It sticks out in my mind because it was one of the only times I ever thought about walking out the door of the client's home and never looking back.

The clients had contacted me because of the violent behavior they were experiencing, such as objects flying off tables, countertops, dressers, and the like. They were terrified, and quite frankly I couldn't blame them.

Anyway, I arrived at the house, and the clients greeted me at the door. The second I stepped into the house I noticed that the energy of the home seemed electrified and chaotic. Before I could get my bearings, a knife flew at me, literally out of nowhere, and penetrated the wooden doorjamb next to my head. The clients shrieked in horror, and at that point I debated with myself whether to stay or go, but only for a second—I knew I had to act fast to calm this situation down.

I took a deep breath and calmly reached up and grabbed the knife, pulling it out the wooden door frame. "Is that the best you got?" I asked out loud to the poltergeist present.

Within a split second, the energy in the house drastically changed; it was like the entire house exhaled. It took a few visits, but eventually the homeowners and I were able to rid the house of the poltergeist.

I don't normally confront a poltergeist in the manner I did in this story, but the situation warranted that I take control of the situation and show no fear. I'm not sure standing up to a poltergeist the way I did intimidates them, but in this case, it calmed the situation down.

I wouldn't recommend provoking a poltergeist in the manner I did, because in some cases the poltergeist could react with extreme violence. Every poltergeist is different, and in the example above I just took a chance.

Some of the techniques in this book, such as smudging, using holy water, and talking to ghosts, have worked, but with poltergeists there's really no guarantee, and you may have to repeat whatever method you choose a few times to get the poltergeist to leave your home.

It's been my experience that smudging (see chapter 6 for more on smudging) is the most effective way to calm the poltergeist down or make the activity stop, at least temporarily. The most effective technique I've found is to keep repeating the smudging as often as you can, daily even, to make the environment for the poltergeist so unbearable that they will simply give up and leave on their own accord.

Purposeful Ghosts

People in the paranormal world widely accept that ghosts with a purpose return for a specific reason and return after death because they are motivated by something they feel is extremely important.

For example, they could return to visit their spouse or children one more time, tell their loved ones where money or important documents are hidden, or warn someone of an impending illness or death. Purposeful ghosts could also be considered messengers, depending on why they've chosen to return.

Purposeful ghosts have a different purpose than avenging ghosts in that they are out to warn the living or convey some type of information. They are normally gentle and kind ghosts, while avenging ghosts are generally angry and filled with rage.

There is nothing to be afraid of if you encounter a ghost with a purpose, as it normally will be the spirit of a loved one or friend who has passed, and if you pay attention, such ghosts will almost always convey an important message to you.

Purposeful ghosts can manipulate a multitude of objects to get their point across, or they may just appear right in front of you and attempt to talk to you. Generally they will communicate using telepathy, so it is important to clear your mind and let the messages come through. You will recognize that the thoughts are not your own and will know it is your purposeful ghost trying to tell you something it feels is important.

They can also use objects to let you know they are there. For example, if you have a picture of them in your house, they might knock the picture over, move the picture, or make the picture appear in different places to let you know who your invisible phantom is.

They can leave other clues as well. They might try to lead you to a particular place to convey their purpose. They do this by making lights blink in a pathway kind of way so you'll follow them, or they might open a drawer where something they need you to see or look closer at is stored, or they might use a radio or television that's on to speak through it directly to give you their message or tell you their purpose for being there.

A purposeful ghost can have other reasons to appear to you. Perhaps its death appeared to be from an accident or suicide, but it was really murder. The purpose of this ghost would then be to tell you it was murdered so you could alert the authorities.

No matter the reason, purposeful ghosts will always have something they feel is important enough that they will try to get your attention and convey their purpose so they can find peace.

Renovation Ghosts

A *renovation ghost* will show up as soon as, or shortly after, you begin home improvements. It's believed that this type of spirit may have been lying dormant for years and is awakened when home or business renovations begin.

This type of entity might hide tools or work materials, or cause other mischievous behavior that can lead you to believe that you have a poltergeist. They might plug in or unplug power tools, appear as apparitions and frighten workers, or move things around.

Renovation ghosts are either happy about the renovations because someone is improving their abode, or they are upset that things are changing around your house (or place of business).

It's very possible that before you began renovations you'd never experienced any type of paranormal activity in your home or business, and then have a boatload of paranormal activity begin as soon as renovations start.

Keep in mind that a renovation ghost can show up even in newer houses. This is because many times the ghost or spirit is tied to the land, not the house. The act of renovating or even building the house in the first place is enough to awaken the ghost that has been dormant in the land itself for, perhaps, hundreds of years.

The easiest way to deal with a renovation ghost is to talk to it calmly and explain that the renovations are necessary to make the building more comfortable, and that you understand that the work is disruptive, but it will all be worth it in the end. Normally having a nice conversation with a renovation ghost will calm things down a bit. Generally, a renovation ghost will show up at the start of renovations and disappear as soon as the home or business remodeling ends.

A friend of mine had to deal with a renovation ghost when he was remodeling the second floor of his house. Tools would be moved; wood would be moved and restacked in different places; extension cords would either be wound or unwound and draped across the room, depending on the mood of the ghost; and footsteps would be heard walking around the second floor at night, as if the ghost was surveying the progress.

Once the project was completed, the ghost was never heard from again—apparently it approved of the modernization of its living space.

Messenger Ghosts

Messenger ghosts are exactly that—their only purpose is to deliver a message to someone they knew when they were alive. The message could be about anything, but whatever the topic, it is important enough to the ghost to hang around until the message is delivered. This message could be a warning of an upcoming illness or death, a goodbye to loved ones and friends, or to tell where something is hidden, among many other reasons.

Messenger ghosts will go out of their way to interact with the living in order to give their message. Once the message is delivered, a messenger ghost will normally cross over to the other side and not return to the world of the living, unless the ghost has another message to give.

Messenger ghosts can appear by their grave, in your home or place of work, and even in your dreams in order to achieve their objective. While most messenger ghosts will appear as a full-body or partial apparition, it's also possible for them to make themselves known in other ways as well. They can cause writing to appear on a computer, a piece of paper, walls, or mirrors, or they might try to speak to you directly.

Messenger ghosts become easily frustrated, because if they appear as a full-body apparition, they generally scare the living daylights out of the person they appear to, and the person will normally scream and flee from the room in terror.

These ghosts are really nothing to fear, and once you get over the shock of seeing a ghost, it will make it easier for the messenger ghost to deliver its message and be on its way.

Some messenger ghosts, or *messengers*, will appear to a loved one to tell them they are fine and to bring comfort to the grieving family member or friend.

Many different types of entities fall under the category of messengers; the most common are family members or friends who have passed away.

Ghosts that want to help the living are always friendly and will go out of their way to find methods of communicating with the living. Angels, guardians, and spirit guides often cannot speak directly to the living but can appear in dreams or try to nudge us in the right direction without interfering with our free will.

Messengers, on the other hand, not only can appear in our dreams to deliver messages, but also may appear as full-body apparitions in order to get their messages delivered.

In the case of a messenger being a loved one, once the message is delivered, they generally will not appear to the living again, unless they find it necessary. In most cases, a messenger will be at peace after it has finished what it felt was important.

Messenger ghosts are normally translucent and generally appear in the same clothing they wore when they were alive. Messengers can be male or female and will appear to living people they knew and trusted when they themselves were alive.

A messenger could also appear in order to warn of an upcoming illness, death, or crisis, or to convey a secret. If you have a messenger ghost in your home or place of business, it does not mean you are being haunted. A messenger ghost is considered a paranormal event or series of events.

These types of ghosts will appear repeatedly until the living understand what the ghost is trying to tell them, and then the ghost will disappear. It's unlikely that once a messenger ghost has delivered its message that it will appear again.

For example, let's assume that someone has died and the family can't locate the deceased person's will, even though they are positive there is one in existence. A messenger ghost could appear to them and tell them where it is, or come to them in a dream to give them the exact location of the will.

It's also possible that the ghost could cause a drawer to open or cause another kind of event that leads the family used in our example to the will.

Many messenger ghosts can also be classified as ghosts that help, because some of the messages they deliver are to help the living. There are several types of messenger ghosts, all with their unique characteristics.

Cemetery Ghosts

A *cemetery ghost*, or *graveyard ghost*, is a type of spirit that is seen around its grave within weeks, days, or months after its death.

These spirits can either appear before they cross over to the other side or choose to visit their body's final resting place. It is possible, although rare, for cemetery ghosts to appear at their grave many years after they've passed away.

Cemetery ghosts may choose to appear by their burial place when a loved one is visiting the graveyard, or they might even appear to perfect strangers.

No one is really sure why spirits choose to appear by their graves. It's actually very rare for a cemetery to be haunted, because the spirit generally didn't have an attachment to the cemetery while alive.

One theory about why spirits will show up at their grave is that they have a message for a family member or friend and are waiting for them to visit the gravesite to deliver that message before crossing over to the other side, or returning to the other side, whatever the case may be.

If you should happen to encounter a graveyard ghost, whether a friend, relative, or stranger, do not be afraid of the ghost. Graveyard ghosts are not there to hurt anyone; they just want to take care of some unfinished business before they rest in peace, and you may be awarded the unique opportunity to help the ghost.

Your best course of action should you encounter a cemetery ghost is to calmly acknowledge it whether you know the ghost or not. You can ask it if it needs help, what it wants, or you can say whatever you're comfortable with as long as it's not said in anger. There is no reason to yell, scream, or ignore a cemetery ghost. Generally a cemetery ghost will communicate with you through telepathy. Think of it as a rare opportunity to help someone, even if they are dead.

Personally I've been fortunate enough to help a cemetery ghost. I was in the local cemetery during the day, doing some genealogical research on some of the founders of my town, when a little old lady approached me.

She was all dressed up and quite frankly looked out of place.

"Can you help me, dear?" she asked telepathically.

Realizing this woman was a ghost and not a living person, I telepathically answered, "What do you need?"

"Do you know who has my cameo brooch?" she replied, her dead eyes gazing hopefully into mine.

"No, I don't. What's your name?" I asked.

"Isabella. I'm buried right over here." She raised a bony finger and pointed to the east.

"Can you show me?" I said.

I followed Isabella as she wafted through the tombstones. She finally stopped at a modest but beautiful tombstone. I recognized her last name as I read the inscription, and was shocked to see she'd been dead for almost ten years.

"You poor thing. You've been wandering around here all this time?" I fought to hold back tears.

"Yes. Can you help me?"

"I'll try," I promised.

A few days later I was attending a historical society function in town and saw that Isabella's daughter, Lisa, was in attendance. I sighed, knowing that I was going to have to ask her about the brooch, and there was no easy way to do it.

After introducing myself, I asked her about her mother's cameo brooch. Her eyes grew wide, and she looked at me suspiciously.

"What about my mother's brooch?" she asked.

Having no other choice, I explained to her who I was and what I did, and then told her about talking to her mother at the cemetery.

"I have the brooch," she said. "But if what you say is true, I'm going to the cemetery with you."

"As you wish," I shrugged. Clearly she wasn't convinced.

Lisa followed me to the cemetery, and when she got out of her car, I saw her mother rush toward her and try to embrace her in a hug. Lisa shivered in the warm weather and commented about the sudden coldness.

"It was your mother hugging you," I explained.

After telling Isabella that Lisa had her brooch, I spent the next hour acting as a liaison between Lisa and her mother, giving them one last chance to say goodbye.

When they finished, Isabella thanked me and faded away. Lisa stood in shocked silence, still trying to wrap her head around what just happened. Then she embraced me in a warm hug and thanked me profusely.

"Just doing my job," I told her. And so ended another day in my life as a medium.

Transitional Ghosts

A *transitional ghost* is a type of spirit that will appear to living family members and/or close friends shortly after the person has passed away. Generally a transitional ghost will appear for only a few moments, and you may hear the voice of the deceased call out your name. It's also possible that this type of ghost will find some other way to communicate.

For example, when my dad was dying, I felt Death the second I walked into my dad's ICU room at the hospital. It's an icy-cold feeling that grips your heart and squeezes.

My dad lay perfectly still in his bed. I could hear the machines and tubes keeping him alive whirling away in the background.

The impersonal, sterile surroundings were a sharp contrast to the warmth I felt when I slipped my hand into his. He held onto me tightly.

He opened his eyes and looked at me. Our eyes met, and a thousand words were silently spoken. We both knew it was time.

How ironic it should end like this, I thought. He'd rescued me from an orphanage when I was just a baby. My mother had wanted a son. My dad a daughter.

Growing up, it was always my dad and I against the world. We'd done everything together: fished, raced cars, camped. My mother always seemed to be an outsider to our world. How was I going to survive without him? My confidant. My best friend.

Now, as it should be, it was just the two of us. My mother sat at home in a wheelchair, waiting for me to call and tell her it was over.

His breathing became irregular, and I sensed Death moving from the corner of the room to the foot of the bed. There wasn't much time.

What do you say to the man who gave you the universe and hung the moon when you know these are the last words he'll ever hear?

Quiet tears began to roll down my cheeks, and I held his hand tighter. "I love you, Daddy," I said.

His hand squeezed mine.

Death then gently took him in its arms and ended his suffering.

I sat, my hand still in his, and watched his face relax, free from the pain and suffering. A warm feeling wrapped around my heart like a blanket when his spirit appeared before me—he looked healthy, his blue eyes twinkled. I then heard his voice in my head say, "It's okay, Sweet Pea. I'm free now. Take care of your mother. I'll always love you." With those words, he faded away.

Normally, as was the case with my dad, this type of ghost just wants you to know they are okay and not to worry about them, although it's possible they could have some other type of message.

Many paranormal researchers believe these types of spirits are similar to messengers, because once their message is conveyed, they will probably not appear again.

Relatives and Friends

Ghosts of relatives and friends attach themselves to a member of their family or a close friend they had when they were alive. Some people in the paranormal field believe that the spirits of ghosts and friends will warn the living about upcoming disasters or deaths.

It's also widely accepted that if you ask your deceased relatives or friends to come into a photograph that is being taken, they may choose to appear in the picture. I've seen this happen many times, but it doesn't always happen, so be patient. If you choose, you could invite your deceased relatives or friends to come into a photograph at special events such as weddings, anniversary parties, birthday parties, etc.

There is no reason to fear the ghosts of relatives or friends; they are basically the same as they were when they were alive and generally mean no harm.

The ghost of a relative or friend could also appear to you in a dream because that is the easiest way for it to convey its message or simply to talk to you without scaring the bejeebers out of you, so pay attention to your dreams.

There are also those in the paranormal field, myself included, who feel it's not healthy for a living person to have a ghost of a departed loved one attaching itself—nor is it healthy for the ghost.

You see, when a person dies, they are supposed to move on to the other side; it's where they belong to carry on in a new plane of existence, and the people they left behind need to grieve and move forward with their lives. It's the natural cycle of life and death.

When a deceased person remains earthbound and doesn't move on, it interferes with the natural order of the universe. The living person left behind is not allowed to grieve properly and move forward with his or her own life, and the deceased person is left in a type of limbo between our world and the other side.

As you can see, this relationship, while it may be comforting for a while, is unhealthy for both parties involved.

While personally never dealing with a case of this nature, I did hear about such a case a few years ago. A woman's husband died and came back to his wife in spirit form. From what I understand, they were still very much in love after years of marriage. This woman and her ghostly husband carried on the day's activities much as they did when he was alive. Apparently, this went on for some years before the children realized what was going on and called in a medium to help their father and mother let go of each other, and to help their father cross over to the other side.

MYSTERIOUS GHOSTS

Mysterious ghosts are entities that are unexplainable because no one really knows exactly what they are or what their purpose is, although there are many theories that paranormal researchers have put forth in an attempt to explain these mysterious phantoms. It's these beings, and the mysteries and theories surrounding them, that will be discussed in this section. They can include *light beings and creatures, orbs, shadow people,* and *elementals.*

While these beings hang around the living, there is little if any attempt on their part to interact with humans, and these creatures are quite controversial in their own right.

Most of the controversy stems from not being able to determine exactly what these beings are. Orbs, for example, are believed to be little balls of energy that normally show up in a picture or video recording; however, most orbs can be dismissed as a bug or a piece of dust.

Light beings and/or creatures also show up frequently on photographs and video and can appear in all types of shapes, sizes, and colors.

Other than orbs, the most commonly reported mysterious creature is shadow people. If you think about it, you've probably seen a few—they are the movement you see out of the corner of your eye, and when you turn to look, there's nothing there.

Light Beings and Creatures

In most cases, these entities that defy explanation are among some of the most mysterious anomalies I've ever encountered during my years as a ghost hunter.

No one is quite sure exactly what they are. Some people believe they are angels, and others believe they are some type of creature from another dimension.

In contrast, there are those who believe they could be fairies, nature spirits, or some other type of living creatures.

Some paranormal researchers believe that they could be an energy vortex or some type of portal opening or closing. They don't appear to have any set pattern and tend to show up just about anywhere at any time.

Generally they aren't visible to the naked eye but instead show up on photographs and video recordings. When light beings are photographed, they show up as bars of light or some other bizarrely shaped light form. On video these creatures tend to move extremely fast and, in some cases, change shape as they move.

By all accounts they seem to be completely harmless and, in my experience, have shown no interest in interacting with the living. Quite frankly, I'm not even sure they know we exist.

Orbs

Orbs are one of the most controversial topics in the paranormal community. It's been estimated that over 80 percent of all apparent orbs that show up in photographs or on video are really nothing more than dust, bugs, dirt, moisture in the air, a lens flare, and/or a reflection.

They tend to show up as transparent balls of light, and some paranormal investigators believe that a true orb will be self-illuminating, meaning they generate their own light and don't use an outside source, such as a camera flash, to show themselves.

There are people who believe that they can see faces peering out at them from the inside of an orb, and I have to admit that I've seen what appears to be a face in many pictures of purported orbs.

However, I don't put much stock in the presence of apparent orbs as evidence of paranormal activity, because they can show up on a photograph simply due to weather conditions or other conditions present at the time the picture was taken.

Yet if true orbs are present and are accompanied by other forms of documented paranormal activity, then they might be worth a second look.

Orbs can show up anywhere, including in your home, a cemetery, or a grocery store. They normally can't be seen with the naked eye, and you can't feel their presence; they are just simply there.

While orbs normally appear as little white balls of light, they have also been photographed in different colors—such as red, blue, purple, pink, or just about any other color—and no one knows how many colors a true orb is capable of producing.

Some people believe that aliens are using orbs as remote viewers in order to spy on Earth. Proponents of this theory believe that aliens are using the orbs because they are virtually invisible, and thus the aliens can spy on us undetected.

Others believe that orbs are angels watching over the living. The followers of this theory believe that angels use orbs to come to Earth to heal the sick or comfort people in times of tragedy, or that they are guardians to protect the weak.

The most widely accepted theory is that orbs are ghosts of people in their most natural state—pure energy. This theory could help explain why people report seeing faces in the middle of an orb when photographed.

Personally, I'm not sure what orbs are or if they are really legitimate as evidence of paranormal activity. If I had to choose a theory, I'd go with the theory that orbs are spirits in their natural form.

A friend of mine tried an experiment with orbs and photography one night. We were out taking pictures, and she noticed a true orb show up in a picture on her digital camera. I then held out my hand and started to coax the orb to land in my hand.

My friend kept taking pictures in rapid succession, and sure enough, the orb flew slowly to my outstretched hand and landed there. While I felt a little rush of energy in my hand, I couldn't see the orb with my naked eye.

Based on this personal experience, I would have to say that the particular orb I encountered interacted with me and therefore could be classified as an intelligent being.

For the most part, orbs seem to be pretty harmless, although there have been cases where an orb has been present, and as it flew by someone, that person was pushed, scratched, or experienced some other type of unseen physical contact.

I'm not sure this can be attributed to the orb or whether there was an actual spirit present. Personally I've never had this type of experience, and until I do, I'll reserve judgment.

Portals

There is much controversy about portals in the paranormal and scientific community. This controversy arises because no one is exactly sure if portals even exist.

Portals are alleged doorways to other dimensions that open and close at will, allowing ghosts, spirits, demons, and just about anything to pass through them into or out of the world of the living.

Portals are mysterious, but they are also benign because they are the equivalent of opening and/or shutting a door in your house, allowing something or someone in or out. However, the ghosts, spirits, or other types of entities that can pass through a portal are not always benign and could actually be quite active.

Some people believe that portals can appear just about anywhere and disappear as quickly as they come. There are others who believe that a portal can be opened or closed by the living who are trained in such things or possess the ability to do so.

Still others believe that portals are holes punched into the energy field that surrounds the planet. While no explanation is given for how these holes are put into the energy field, it is a possibility, especially given global warming and other planetary and human forces on Earth.

There are scientists who feel it's impossible for a portal to exist. However, science has proved that other dimensions exist, so why isn't it possible that beings of some kind can pass from one dimension to another? To do that, they could use a portal as a means of transportation.

Many paranormal researchers believe mirrors can be a type of portal from the world of the living to the world of the dead, or the "other side," as it is most commonly referred to. A portal that opens or closes in a mirror would be due to some type of human interaction. (I have more to say about mirrors in chapter 4.)

A good example of a portal is illustrated by the use of a Ouija board. When someone uses a Ouija board and invites ghosts and/or spirits into their home, they are opening a door, or portal, between the world of the living and the world of the dead, allowing anything—good or evil—to pass through it.

Shadow People

Have you ever seen something move or a shadowy figure out of the corner of your eye and turned around and no one was there? More than likely, it was a shadow person.

A shadow person is just what the name implies: the shadow of a person, except there's no person there who can cause the shadow. Shadow people tend to be very shy and most of the time will race out of the room at the speed of light when detected. They appear to be harmless and generally make no attempt to interact with the living.

Shadow people tend to come in all shapes and sizes, just like living people, and can appear opaque or rather solid, but normally with very little detail. Most of the time you can only tell if it's a man or a woman, or, if you get lucky, you may be able to distinguish a rough outline of clothing.

While sightings of shadow people are very common, they are one of the most mysterious types of entities in existence. No one is quite sure of their purpose, but, as you can imagine, theories abound.

Some paranormal researchers think that shadow people are a type of demon because there have been reports of shadow people with red eyes, appearing as a dark form, instead of the usual misty white of other types of ghosts.

Other people have reported malevolent feelings in the presence of a shadow person. Personally I've never experienced these feelings off a true shadow person. It could be that some people are mistaking a shadow person for a type of negative entity or another type of ghost or spirit.

Another popular theory is that shadow people are watchers and are simply observing life on Earth. However, no one really knows if they are beings from another dimension or a type of ghost of a person who is deceased, or for that matter if they've ever been alive in the sense that we are alive.

For example, I have a shadow person who shows up occasionally in my home and seems to be fascinated with going up and down the stairs to the second floor. Don't ask me why; I haven't a clue. All I know about my spectral visitor is that it is a man, a rather large man. I can see his fingers on the white stair railing when he is coming down the stairs, and the second he realizes that I've seen him, he darts out the front door at lightning speed.

My shadow person has never made any attempt to communicate or interact with me and gives the distinct impression that he is more afraid of me than I am of him, although that's not hard to do because most ghosts don't frighten me in the least.

To my knowledge there is no way to get rid of a shadow person—and since they appear to be rather benign, you probably don't have to worry about one being around your house.

Elementals

This type of entity can cover a wide range of possible types of spirits and cause what many people believe are hauntings.

People tend to agree that *elementals* are nature spirits, and the belief in elementals in Ireland, Scotland, and other parts of Europe is very common. Creatures such as gremlins, leprechauns, pixies, or fairies can fall under this category. There are people who would say that these types of creatures are nothing but myth or legend, but to a lot of people they are extremely real, and these people go out of their way not to anger or disturb these entities for fear of harsh retribution.

Some religions view elementals as types of spirits that rule nature, and they believe there are fire, earth, air, and water elementals that each have different characteristics.

In Animism, which is believed to be the first religion of humanity, elementals were present in everything on Earth;

belief in elementals was once common—until the Catholic Church convinced many people that elementals didn't exist because they couldn't be seen.

One theory among some paranormal researchers is that elementals have to be summoned to carry out specific duties and will continue to perform those duties until the person who summoned them sends them away.

It's widely believed in many circles that elementals are negative entities that can cause great harm to the living because they are born from Earth's elements. I'm not convinced that all elementals are negative, but I do think that they could be, in many cases, protecting something or someone and will take extreme measures to carry out this task. Does this make them bad?

As far as I know, there is only one documented case of an elemental, and that's at Leap Castle in Ireland. No one really knows how the elemental came to exist in the castle; however, Mildred Darby, one of the owners of the castle in the late nineteenth century, may have been the first to come across the elemental.

In 1909, Mildred Darby wrote an article for the journal *Occult Review* in which she describes the paranormal entity that she invoked, strictly by accident. She says that she felt someone put a hand on her shoulder, and when she turned around she saw the entity. She goes on to say that the being was about the size of a sheep and thin, gaunt, and shadowy. It had a face and eyes that seemed to be partially decomposed in black eye sockets, and it stared at her intently. She says this being was accompanied by a horrid smell, akin to a decomposing corpse.

SPIRITS THAT HARM

A number of ghosts can cause psychological and physical injury to the living. Most of these types of phantoms are known as *inhumans*, meaning they were never alive in human form. But a particularly nasty spirit could cause one to believe they have a demon, because demons are capable of great harm both physically and psychologically.

Spirits that harm are mostly inhumans—such as *demons*, *incubi*, and *succubi*—although there are malevolent ghosts that can cause harm as well. It appears that these spirits' only goal is to cause great upheaval in the lives of the living, and in some cases, they will go to great lengths to do so. They can attack you psychologically, emotionally, and physically, leaving a path of destruction in their wake.

These types of entities, in most cases, are out to do nothing but make your life a living hell, and they are capable of carrying out this mission in unique and terrifying ways.

Demons

Demons are some of the most insidious, evil, and vile entities I've ever run into in all my years of ghost hunting. They are capable of wrecking unbelievable psychological and physical damage to the living. Don't believe in demons? I didn't either—until I ran headfirst into one. So I'm speaking from personal experience.

There have been reports of demons causing physical injuries, such as scratches and welt and bite marks, to their intended victims and their families.

The presence of a demon may be accompanied by a foul odor that resembles rotten eggs, sulfuric acid, or rotting flesh, or, in some cases, an audible growl that sounds like an extremely large dog.

They can make the air in a room feel thick and heavy, or they can cause the room to become icy cold or sweltering hot, depending on their mood at that particular moment.

Demons have also been known to make verbal threats, throw things, move furniture in a violent manner, push you, throw you, scratch you, bite you, and do any number of other violent acts to terrify you.

However, a demon's most powerful weapon is psychological warfare. Demons are known to cause overwhelming feelings of fear, anxiety, anger, and a whole range of other negative emotions—all to weaken their prey so they become easier for the demon to control. The more chaos and emotional upheaval they can cause in a person's life, the more powerful they become.

This type of negative phantom can target one person or an entire family. They can put thoughts into people's heads that could make them act out in a violent and/or negative manner that is totally out of character.

Some demons will try to isolate their prey so that the only thing this person can rely on is the demon. A person under attack by a demon may start to withdraw, and verbally or physically attack their family members and friends. It's important to remember that this is not about possession; it's about control.

Demons can be attracted to people who are suffering from a mental illness, are depressed, or are very emotional. They are also attracted to households that are in a constant state of upheaval and stress, in which people are frequently yelling and fighting with each other. Some paranormal researchers believe that demons feed in some way off of this negative energy and become stronger and more powerful.

While demons can't make us do anything, because we have free will, they will try to entice their victims or persuade them to do their bidding. Demons are very cunning and seem to have the uncanny ability to instinctively know one's weaknesses. They use these weaknesses or greatest fears to put their victims in an emotionally and psychologically unstable state of mind, so they can gain control over them.

Demons can also appear to be the ghost of a child or a loved one who has passed away. They do this in an attempt to gain your trust and make you put your guard down. This makes it much easier for them to insinuate themselves into your life.

As I mentioned, this type of entity in the paranormal world is referred to as an *inhuman* and was never alive in human form like you and me. They are also one of the hardest types of entities to get rid of.

Many people believe that demons mark you in some way that enables them to find you no matter where you are, anytime they want.

Members of certain religions and some paranormal researchers believe that speaking the name of a demon could summon the demon, making it more powerful.

I don't necessarily agree with this line of thought, however. I tend to believe that if you speak the name of the demon, it gives you a little bit of power over the demon, because it lets the demon know that you are aware of who it is and, more importantly, *what* it is.

I believe that by calling out the demon's name, it may keep the demon somewhat honest. It lets these types of entities know that you are not fooled by their attempt at trickery and that you are aware of exactly what they are.

In some cases, this fact alone can give you a tiny bit of control over them and the situation. It can make you feel empowered because you saw through their act.

If you believe that your house has been invaded by a demon, don't attempt to get rid of it on your own. You won't win and could only end up making the demon angry, which could lead to great physical and emotional harm to you and your family.

You should immediately seek the help of a qualified paranormal researcher or a trusted member of the clergy if you believe you or your family has fallen victim to a demonic entity.

My friend Alexis McQuillan encountered a rather nasty demon a few years ago. This demon would attack her in bed while she was sleeping and did everything it could to isolate her. Thankfully, Alexis was able to get rid of the demon in a way, but it still haunts her. You can read more about Alexis's adventure in her book, *Encounter with Hell*.

Incubi and Succubi

Incubi and succubi are included in the demon/inhuman category. An incubus is considered to be a specific type of male demon whose mission is to have sex with living women. Its counterpart, the succubus, is a female demon that attacks men in order to have sex with them.

The tales of the incubus and succubus date back hundreds if not thousands of years, and some of the most popular tales of bygone days included writings that incubi and succubi were demons that could change their gender; they were allegedly able to take semen from a man and then change into an incubus and impregnate a woman.

In some religions, it is believed that if an incubus or succubus visits the same person repeatedly over a period of time, then it can cause the living person to not only become very sick but also die.

Tales of people being attacked by an incubus or succubus continue to this day, and sometimes it's hard to separate whether these people were attacked or are simply suffering from sleep paralysis.

Sleep paralysis is caused during the REM state of sleep, when your body releases hormones that paralyze your body to prevent it from acting out during dreams, in order to reduce the likelihood of injury while sleeping.

Most of the time, these hormones wear off before you wake up, but in some cases people wake up and are temporarily paralyzed and can feel as though they are in the presence of an evil spirit and are being attacked.

People who have suffered an attack—be it by an incubus or a succubus or by sleep paralysis—will swear they were attacked by a demon, and in many cases doctors write off this apparent attack as sleep paralysis when in fact it's possible the person was actually attacked by one of these menacing demons.

The owner of an inn in England claims to be visited by a succubus at least once a week. He claims that while he is sleeping, this demon attacks him and tries to have intercourse with him.

Parasitic Entities

Parasitic entities will attach themselves to living people in order to suck out their life energy like a giant vacuum. Also known as *spirit attachment*, there are different types of entities that will leech onto people.

It's widely accepted in paranormal circles that most of these parasitic entities were once human and alive, although in some cases the entity could be in the form of a demon. Either way, they are extremely dangerous and harmful to the living person they've attached themselves to.

Symptoms associated with a parasitic entity include lack of motivation, dizziness, weakness, the inability to think clearly, addiction to certain drugs or activities, unusual and extreme tiredness, restless sleep, and extreme nightmares.

If you're experiencing some of these symptoms, don't automatically jump to the conclusion that it is a parasitic entity. It's very possible you are suffering from some type of physical or psychological ailment, and you should consult your doctor to rule out any natural cause for how you're feeling.

If a parasitic entity is allowed to continue to suck the life out of you, your body won't be strong enough to fight off a simple illness, and in some extreme cases, the body will die and the parasitic entity will move on to its next victim. More details about spirit attachment can be found in chapter 4.

× × ×

I can't state how strongly I believe that you should never try by yourself to get rid of any of the types of entities described in the previous section. These types of phantoms are extremely dangerous and are capable of doing irreparable harm to you or someone you care about. Professional help from a qualified paranormal investigator and/or a member of clergy could be your only chance of getting rid of them.

The emotional and psychological scars these types of entities can leave in their wake are almost beyond human compre-
hension. They can leave you broken, emotionally and
psychologically drained, and a mere shell of the person you
were before these evil phantoms came into your life.

As an example, let's say you've not been feeling well lately
or haven't felt like yourself. You go to the doctor numerous
times and undergo a mountain of tests, but the doctor finds
nothing wrong with you physically. Yet you feel sapped of
strength and emotionally drained, and your friends have
noticed a change in your behavior—not a good change.
Chances are you could have a parasitic entity attached to you.

SPIRITS THAT HELP

Ghosts that want to help the living are always friendly and
will go out of their way to find methods of communicating
with the living. Angels, guardians, and spirit guides often
cannot speak directly to the living, but can appear in dreams
or try to nudge us in the right direction without interfering
with our free will and freedom of choice.

While there are many different types of spirits that can
help you with various things, such as messengers, for the
purpose of this book I've put specific types of entities into
this category because they have no ulterior motive, such as to
deliver a message. Their only purpose is to help the living in
many ways.

Angelic Beings

In much of recorded history and even today, many people have reported encounters with angelic beings. Most of these reports seem to have a common thread in that the angel has visited them in some manner.

Some paranormal investigators and others view angels as messengers who carry words from God to the intended person. Often an angelic being will appear when a living person is experiencing a difficult time in their life, in order to bring that person comfort and hope.

People who have reported meeting angels have also stated that angels generally appear in human form and can be accompanied by certain scents, such as rose, sandalwood, and pine, as well as a visual increase in color intensity, particularly blue and green.

Believers who study angelic encounters say that an angel could also appear as a winged being or a child, friend, or family member who is deceased.

Many people believe that a specific type of angel, called a *guardian angel*, is assigned to a person when they are born in order to gently guide and protect them throughout their life. These people say that a guardian angel could be a deceased family member or an ascended soul.

I heard a story somewhere that if you find little white feathers around your house in obvious places, and you're sure they aren't from a down blanket or pillow, then they are a gift from your guardian angel to let you know they are there and watching over you.

An angelic being can appear as a bright light that doesn't hurt your eyes. This light could be accompanied by nurturing feelings of unconditional comfort, love, safety, and contentment. This type of being can also be present and cause these feelings without showing itself to you.

If you encounter an angelic being, there is nothing for you to fear. It is simply there to make you feel better or to bring you a message. Once its mission is accomplished, it will leave on its own and may or may not return at some point, depending on if it is needed again.

I read about a case recently in which a woman had lost her husband suddenly in an accident. She was devastated and wracked with grief. She spent a few weeks in her bedroom, barely eating, not showering or getting dressed—she wanted to die so she could be with her husband.

Then one night she reported that her entire bedroom filled up with a bright white light and that this light moved toward her, slowly turning into the outline of a man. She became very scared, but a man's voice popped into her head and said, "Don't be afraid. I'm here to help you." With those words, he moved forward and enveloped her in the light. She said she never felt in her life more unconditional love, peace, and acceptance.

When this being moved away, he said, "Your husband is with us. He is fine and wants you to move on with your life, not to grieve, because he is among the angels."

The woman said she fell into a deep sleep and the next morning felt renewed, refreshed, and ready to move forward with her life. She firmly believes the being that visited her was an angel helping her in her grief.

Just take comfort in the fact that an angelic being is watching over you and that you're never alone, even in your darkest hours.

Guardians

People of certain religions believe entities called *guardians* or *watchers*, not to be confused with angels or guardian angels, are a particular type of entity sent to watch over and protect women, typically at the onset of menopause.

It's very rare to see a guardian, but some women report that they've seen a large, robed figure with a hood over its head to hide its face. It may sound scary, but guardians are very kind and gentle to those they are sent to watch over and have been known to take extreme measures to take care of the woman they've vowed to protect.

Guardians are not there to interfere with a woman's life, but rather to help, guide, and protect her throughout the rest of her life, and then accompany her to the other side when she dies to ensure the transition from life to death goes smoothly. They comfort the woman during this time.

I can't help but feel sorry for my guardian because, being a ghost hunter, I put myself into some potentially dangerous situations—not something my guardian would approve of, I'm sure.

One night I was out ghost hunting with a friend of mine. Because the cemetery we were investigating was quite large, we decided to separate but keep within eyesight of each other.

As I walked among the tombstones, I became lost in thought and really wasn't paying attention to where I was walking—a cardinal mistake for a ghost hunter. I tripped over a small tombstone and landed hard on my chest and stomach, knocking the breath out of me.

As I lay there gasping for air, I sensed a presence and looked up to find a robed being standing over me, his face obscured by the hood of his robe. He extended a hand to me and I took it, noticing how warm and safe I felt with his hand wrapped around mine. He helped me to my feet and then faded away.

That was my guardian helping me and, I believe, telling me to be more careful in the future.

Spirit Guides

It is believed that, like guardian angels, spirit guides are given to us at the time of birth and stay with us for our entire lives, coming and going as we face certain situations.

Spiritualists and many New Age believers feel that spirit guides have a level of consciousness that is a step above some other beings in the spiritual realm and could be ascended masters, or normal spirits that excel in particular areas and are best equipped to help us deal with a specific situation in our lives.

While they are not allowed to interfere directly with our lives due to the fact that we as humans have free will, they *are* allowed to give us signs to make us pay attention to something. These signs could be a string of coincidences that you can't ignore, so it's important to pay attention to things when you notice them—especially if something happens that you normally wouldn't pay attention to. This means that there's a message there for you somewhere; you just have to look for it.

For example, have you ever experienced that feeling in the pit of your stomach when facing a choice, or you're in some type of situation you're not sure of? It would be wise to listen to your gut because generally that is one of your spirit guides trying to nudge you in the right direction.

CHAPTER THREE

WHAT KIND OF HAUNTING IS IT?

Many paranormal researchers believe that the energy from events in the past is absorbed into materials such as stone, wood, or just about any other porous material. There have been cases where material from destroyed buildings is used to construct new buildings, and the residual energy from events that took place in the destroyed building continues on and is often perceived as paranormal activity in the new building.

A *true*, or *intelligent*, haunting has very specific characteristics. First, the paranormal activity must be consistent. If the activity in your home or business is only occasional, then you are not experiencing a haunting; you are experiencing paranormal activity. There is a distinct difference.

Second, in an intelligent haunting the ghost will make an attempt to communicate or interact with the living in some way. This way differs depending on the type of spirit you're dealing with, but generally it will look directly at you, try to talk to you, or do something else so there is no mistaking the ghost is acknowledging you in some way.

Some ghosts and spirits seem to crave attention and acknowledgement and will do just about anything to let you know they're present. For example, they may turn lights on and off, change the channel on the television, or appear before you. They aren't doing this to scare you; they're doing it so you will say hi to them, or to get some kind of reaction out of you.

There's really no reason to be afraid of this type of activity, and in most cases, the ghosts and/or spirits don't mean to scare you; they are just letting you know they are there. It would be nice to acknowledge their presence; in many cases, once you do, they will be content and leave you alone … until the next time.

No two hauntings are alike, just as no two living people are exactly alike. The same principle applies to ghosts. The easiest way to try to figure out what kind of haunting you may be experiencing is to keep a journal of all the paranormal activity that occurs in your home or business.

Write down the date, time, weather conditions, who was present in the home at the time of the event, and whether anyone else was witness to the event. Then write down everything you can remember about the event itself. Make sure to include such things as what you were doing at the time, exactly what happened, and whether you noticed any sounds and smells associated with the activity.

Ask the other members of the family about any paranormal experiences they have had and record the same information as above. It's very important to keep the lines of communication open among people living in the home about the paranormal activity that is happening. Many times family members won't share their experiences without being asked, because they don't want to upset or scare anyone else in the household.

Many types of entities, such as malevolent spirits and demons, count on the lack of communication so they can isolate family members from each other and eventually gain control of the household. By communicating every day about any paranormal experiences that happen, you are taking away some of a negative entity's power to influence and control the people living in your home.

In addition, keeping a journal can be very helpful not only in determining if you have a residual, intelligent, or other type of haunting, but also in helping to identify what kind of spirit you have, so you'll know how to handle the situation properly and get rid of the unwanted house guest.

Some people tend to forget that a ghost, in most cases, was once a living person and had their own unique personality when alive and that this personality carries over in death.

If a person was a practical joker when they were alive, chances are you're in for a real treat if that ghost decides to haunt your home, so be prepared for a string of practical jokes from your spectral visitor. This situation can actually be quite amusing, and there's no reason to be scared. It's their own unique way of letting you know who is in your home.

In my case, the practical joker is my dad. When alive, he was very fond of electrical gadgets, and this fascination with technology has continued after his death. My husband, also fond of technology, installed wall switches in our house that control the ceiling fan and lights—turning them on and off and dimming them as well.

I will be sitting in my office writing, and all of a sudden the light on the ceiling fan will go real bright, then very dim, then bright again, and then almost to darkness.

Not missing a beat, I will say, "Dad, I thought you said reading in darkness was bad for your eyes?" Well, that's all it takes; the ceiling fan comes back on to full brightness, and I swear I hear my dad chuckling at the same time. "Thanks, Dad. I love you too," I say, and the activity will stop. It's just my dad's way of saying that he's here and he loves me, which is really kind of comforting.

Most paranormal investigators agree that there are three main types of haunting and that they each have their own individual characteristics and share some common denominators.

RESIDUAL HAUNTING

A residual haunting is not caused by a ghost at all; it's caused by a moment in time getting caught up in some type of time warp, and it keeps replaying itself over and over like a video caught in a continuous play loop.

In many cases in which a residual haunting is present, the event replayed is normally a tragic one, such as a murder or a horrific accident of some sort, although it can also be something mundane, such as someone walking up the stairs—an activity that would have been repeated many, many times in a person's life.

Some paranormal researchers believe that a residual haunting is a form of energy that stays in one location. People who experience a residual haunting may see people, animals, or other things interacting with the environment the way it was in the past. You might see what appears to be a ghost walk through a wall or a window. This means that at the time the event happened, there was probably once a doorway there. You could also experience odors or hear someone walk up and/or down stairs or down a hallway, or hear doors opening and closing. Because many residual hauntings are visual, it's easy to see how someone would think they are seeing a ghost, which can of course be very scary to people.

The difference between a residual haunting and a true haunting is clear; in a residual haunting there is no attempt to communicate with the living, and there is no ghost present. In a true, or intelligent, haunting, there is a ghost present and interaction of some sort with the living. A residual haunting may occur only on specific days, or it could appear every day or several times a week at the same time.

You can't make a residual haunting stop or go away. A residual haunting could fade away over time or continue forever. It's important to remember, though, that a residual haunting is perfectly harmless and that there is nothing to be afraid of.

I myself have been a witness to a residual haunting. It occurred many years ago when my husband and I moved into our first home. Every April in the early morning hours, we'd hear a very loud crash in the basement. It sounded as if something metallic were hitting the concrete floor. We'd jump out of bed and race down to the basement, only to find nothing out of place.

This made us crazy until one day I decided to ask my dad about the noise. He'd grown up in the house and would probably know what was causing the noise. He told me that my grandfather had been a mushroom farmer, and every April he had to plow the fields.

The plow he used was suspended by a rope in the rafters of the basement ceiling. He would let the plow fall to the concrete and then back the horses up to the large window in the back of the basement, hitch up the horses, and have them pull the plow out the basement window.

So from that point on, every April when we'd hear the plow fall, we'd laugh and say Grandpa was plowing the fields. Funny how when you know what something is, it takes away any fear.

INTELLIGENT HAUNTING

When people think of a haunting in the traditional sense, this is the type of haunting they are referring to. In reality, an intelligent haunting is quite rare.

An intelligent haunting does involve a ghost or spirit, and generally these types of hauntings are very active and will attempt to interact and/or acknowledge the living. The ghost involved in an intelligent haunting could be choosing a particular location for any number of reasons.

For example, a spirit could be attached to the site where it died as a result of a murder, accident, or other traumatic event; or a ghost could have what it perceives to be unfinished business it feels it needs to complete before crossing over.

A ghost could also come back to haunt its home or place of business, or to stay with friends and loved ones it knew while alive.

In extreme cases, the person may have died in their sleep and not realize they are dead. Personally, these are the hardest cases for me to deal with because I have to gently tell the ghost that they have died and need to cross over into the light.

There have been documented cases where a family member or other loved one does not want to let the person who died go, and is inadvertently keeping that ghost tied to the earth, or earthbound, as it is commonly referred to in the paranormal community. This can cause great stress on the person who died because they want to go into the light but can't.

While it's perfectly acceptable and encouraged to mourn the death of someone you cared about deeply, prolonged mourning is unhealthy not only for the living but also for the person who died. In fact, it can actually be quite cruel even though that's not the intention of the living person. A person who has died belongs on the other side, and holding them here keeps the soul of the deceased person in a world between the living and the dead—something I'm sure no one wants for their loved one.

Other common causes for an intelligent haunting are that the spirit believes some injustice was done to it while alive; it could fear judgment on the other side for things it did while alive; or the ghost could be haunting a home because it believes it needs to protect a person or a secret.

Normally, an intelligent haunting is accompanied by a lot of paranormal activity. This could include lights turning on and off, doors slamming or opening and closing, doors and/ or windows being locked or unlocked, voices, sounds, a scent, the feeling that someone is touching you—or you may see the ghost appear as a mist or even a full-body apparition, as well as a multitude of other types of paranormal activity.

Intelligent, or traditional, hauntings are almost always caused by active ghosts, but specters that fall under the category of inhumans can also be culprits in this type of haunting.

Ghosts generally associated with a traditional haunting can be benign, benevolent, and malevolent. A benign spirit will simply go about its business and really not cause any harm, although it could appear as a full-body apparition and give you a good scare.

A benevolent spirit is very kind and will not do anything to cause harm to those living in a dwelling, and some have been known to protect people or warn of impending danger.

Malevolent spirits are generally mean and nasty, and their only goal is to cause harm in some manner to the living. While many malevolent spirits are demonic in nature, there are spirits that are just mean. Malevolent spirits could be avengers seeking justice or revenge against someone they believed wronged them when they were alive, or they could just be mean toward any living person.

Some people believe that, in some cases, malevolent spirits are jealous of the living because they themselves are no longer alive. Although this is possible, there could be other reasons a ghost is acting in a malevolent manner.

One of the easiest ways to tell if you have a residual or intelligent haunting is to try to communicate with the ghost.

For example, on a recent case, I could feel the ghost there, but it didn't want to communicate with me on a telepathic level. So I took my electromagnetic detector and placed it on a table across the room and then retreated as far away as I could get from it without leaving the room. I explained to the spirit that if it moved past the device, different-colored lights would light up. One light for yes, two lights for no.

I then started asking a series of questions, and each time, either one light or two lights would light up in response.

This is a classic example of a traditional haunting because the ghost in that home communicated with the living, and according to the homeowners, the paranormal activity was consistent.

DEMONIC HAUNTING

A demonic haunting is very much like a traditional haunting except the phantom responsible is an inhuman—remember, by *inhuman* I mean never alive in human form. This could mean that the haunting is being caused by an incubus, succubus, elemental, or demon.

A demonic haunting can make a traditional haunting look like a walk in the park on a sunny summer day. Demons are some of the most insidious, vile, and evil creatures that can invade your home or place of business.

What's more, demons are cunning and sly and can appear as just about anything they want—from the ghost of a loved one to a small child. They do this in order to gain your trust and make you put your guard down.

The entity in this type of haunting is generally attracted to a household that is filled with negative emotions, such as anger and jealously, addiction issues, and homes that are in a state of constant chaos.

Some paranormal researchers believe that demons need to be summoned or invited into a location before they can take up residence there. I agree that trying to summon a demon is never a good idea, but I also believe that demons are capable of finding and attaching themselves to certain people regardless of whether they were summoned or not.

Some people who are experiencing a haunted house will automatically jump to the conclusion that the paranormal activity is being caused by a demon or other type of inhuman entity.

It's easy to confuse some traditional hauntings with demonic hauntings because they behave almost exactly the same. You may experience cold spots, rapping on walls and/or doors and windows, footsteps, foul odors, and in extreme cases you could be punched, pushed, scratched, and physically and/or sexually assaulted.

While a traditional haunting can be terrifying, a demonic haunting takes the activity generally associated with a traditional haunting and bumps it up to the next level.

The more fear, terror, emotional upheaval, and psychological trauma demons and other inhumans can evoke in the living, the more they like it and the more powerful they become. Demons and many other inhumans actually feed off of the fear of the living and become unbelievably powerful.

For example, a demonic entity may scratch, bite, punch, and carry out other physical attacks in order to gain control over you. When a demon scratches, it is normally three claw-like marks. Many paranormal researchers and members of clergy believe three scratches is the sign of the trilogy and the demon is mocking God.

If you believe you have a demon in your house, I wouldn't recommend even attempting to get rid of it yourself. You should immediately contact a reputable paranormal investigator who is experienced in dealing with demons, or a member of clergy.

IS YOUR HOUSE HAUNTED, OR ARE YOU HAUNTED?

Although it doesn't happen very often, it is possible for a spirit to attach itself to a person, in the sense that the person the ghost attaches to is haunted, not the house they live in.

Not all types of spirits can or will attach themselves to a person, but the ghosts most likely to attach to a person include incubi, succubi, and avengers. In extremely rare cases, a poltergeist will attach itself to a person, but generally a poltergeist haunts a location, not just one specific person in that location.

Just because a ghost attaches itself to a living person does not mean that person is possessed. Possession is a totally different thing and involves a spirit or ghost actually taking over the body and thoughts of a living person; a ghost that attaches itself to a person isn't capable of that.

One of the easiest ways to determine if a ghost has attached itself to a living person is to keep track of who is in the room when paranormal activity occurs. Chances are if the same person is always present when the activity occurs, and the paranormal activity doesn't occur when that person isn't in the room, then that person may have a ghost or spirit attached to them.

If you believe a ghost has attached itself to you or a loved one, you should seek the help of a qualified paranormal investigator to help you determine what type of spirit it is, in order to figure out the best way to deal with that ghost and get it to detach and leave you alone.

Some people aren't comfortable contacting someone they don't know in this type of situation, so if you feel more comfortable contacting a trusted member of clergy, they may be able to help you as well. As always, you are free to contact me at debichestnut@yahoo.com.

× × ×

I feel I need to say a few words about haunted locations, because some people jump to the wrong conclusions when dealing with a haunting.

First, I want you to know that there's no reason to live in terror and suffer in silence if you believe your house is haunted. Help is available to you; all you have to do is reach out and ask for it.

You need to not worry whether people will think you're crazy, especially if you believe you are being threatened by any type of paranormal entity. Television has thrust the world of the paranormal into the mainstream, and gone are most of the stigmas involved in admitting your home could be haunted.

Moreover, not every haunting involves a demonic entity. To this day I don't know why some people automatically jump to this conclusion. Truth be told, a demonic haunting is extremely rare, and in my thirty years as a ghost hunter I've only encountered two demonic entities…not experiences I want to repeat anytime soon.

The truth of the matter is that by assuming you have a demonic entity in your home or business, you could actually inadvertently summon a demon to take up residence there. Trust me on this—you don't ever want that to happen.

Finally, for some reason that's still a mystery to me, many people jump to the conclusion that their haunting is caused by their house or place of business being built on top of, or in the area of, a Native American graveyard. This too is very rare, and I've never encountered a home built on top of a Native American cemetery. I have, however, encountered many that are near Native American burial sites, and I myself have lived in a home surrounded by five Native American burial grounds. But I've never encountered a home near one of those sites that was haunted by a Native American, although there's no reason to discount the possibility of such a haunting occurring elsewhere.

CHAPTER FOUR

HOW DID THE GHOST GET HERE?

Have you ever wondered why a ghost or spirit will choose a particular location to haunt instead of the many other places it could choose to go? In other words, "How the heck did the ghost get here?"

Unfortunately, there's no easy answer to that question, but there are a multitude of possibilities. Sometimes, knowing why the ghost is there makes it easier to get rid of said spirit. So let's explore some of the many reasons why a ghost might haunt a particular location.

PAST OWNER OF HOME

Many of the cases I've worked on as a paranormal investigator have involved the ghosts of former owners who aren't quite ready to give up their home. There are generally three reasons why a former owner of a house still occupies it after death.

The first and most common reason is that they don't realize they're dead and are really very confused as to why all their things are gone and strangers are living in their home.

The ghost of a deceased homeowner can appear to be quite violent in that they may throw things, yell at you to get out, turn lights on and off, and exhibit other similar behaviors. While at first glance you may think this is a malevolent spirit, it's really just a frustrated homeowner. Imagine how you would feel if you didn't know you were dead and strangers were living in your home.

If you know who the former owner is, or you've researched the property and found out that information, you can then address the ghost by name and gently tell them that they have died and need to move on to heaven or the other side to be at peace.

The second reason a former owner may haunt what was once their house is because they loved it so much and have fond memories of events that occurred there when they were alive.

If you suspect this is the case with your ghost, then nicely explain that you love the house as much as they did and you will take good care of it, but that it's time they leave and join their loved ones. Normally this will take care of the problem, but you might have to repeat this process a couple of times.

On a personal note, when my grandmother died, the new owners of her beloved home called my mom to tell her that the window blinds were being pulled up and down and that no matter what they put on top of the refrigerator it would be violently thrown off.

My mom told me what was going on and told me to go over to Grandma's old house and "take care of it." Not wanting my grandmother to spend eternity being upset—heaven knows she was a nervous enough woman in life—I drove over to the house.

My grandmother hated taking her pills and kept them on top of the refrigerator, so it was easy to explain why she would throw things off the top of the fridge, and I knew from experience that she was always fussing with the blinds.

When I got to the house I introduced myself to the new owners and, upon entering the home, immediately sensed my grandmother's presence.

"Grandma, you don't have to worry anymore. These nice people will take good care of your house just like you did. You don't have to take your pills anymore, so please quit throwing everything off the top of the fridge. Why don't you go be with Grandpa and your other relatives on the other side?" I said.

"Debi, I'm so confused," Grandma said to me telepathically.

"I know, Grandma, its okay. Do you see a bright white light?" I asked.

"Yes."

"Good. Just walk toward that light, and everyone will come out to meet you. I love you, Grandma," I told her.

"Love you, too," she said.

A couple of minutes later I felt her presence fade away, and I knew she was where she was supposed to be.

I assured the homeowners that she was gone and thanked them for calling us. As far as I know, there has been no more reported paranormal activity at Grandma's old house.

The third reason the ghost of a previous owner might be in your home is they simply don't want to leave. This could be for a multitude of reasons, but normally they feel they have to protect the house and/or some old family secret no one really cares or even knows about, yet it's important to them.

I dealt with the ghost of an owner of a property who died in 1887 and was still walking the rooms of his home. He did this not because he was particularly fond of the house but because he believed he had to protect a huge family secret—how his daughter died at the tender age of twenty under what a local newspaper called "mysterious circumstances."

TIED TO THE LAND

In some cases a ghost or spirit is tied to the land, not the house that's sitting on it. This happens when the ghosts or spirits were, in all likelihood, haunting the house they lived in when they were alive and that house was torn down at some point. This also explains how a totally new house can appear to be haunted when, in reality, the house isn't haunted —the land it sits on is.

In many cases, ghosts that are tied to the land won't even acknowledge the living, but go about their daily activities as they did when they were alive. This leads many paranormal researchers to believe that what is really occurring is a residual haunting, not an actual ghostly haunting.

However, there are cases in which a ghost tied to the land will not only interact with the living but also go out of their way to do so. It's hard to say why they do this, but the two most common theories are that they want the current residents out of what they perceive to be their own house, or they simply want the living to know they are there and to be acknowledged.

For example, it isn't uncommon to hear reports of people seeing apparitions walking through a wall. What this really is, is the ghost or residual energy walking through what used to be a doorway in the dwelling they once lived in.

In extremely rare cases, a parcel of land can be haunted because there's a long-forgotten cemetery or burial ground located on the property. It wasn't unusual in previous eras for people to bury their loved ones on their property. Over the years, people move and the graves are left there—so the graves can stay there undisturbed for years, often without a marker. Once the land is disturbed, even if the graves aren't bothered, it's possible for the ghosts of the people buried there to be awakened from their deathly slumber and start roaming around.

If there's a Native American burial site on the property—again, extremely rare—and the property is disturbed in any manner, the ghosts of the Native Americans buried there could view the disturbance as a violation of sacred land. When this happens, the ghosts tend to be a little more aggressive than usual.

If there's an old well on your property, you will want to have the well filled in. There have been cases where demons use old wells like an open doorway to come onto your property and eventually invade your home.

I'm not sure that filling in the well with rocks, stones, or cement is enough to stop a determined demon, but it's sure worth taking the precaution. Demons, ghosts, and other entities generally will take the path of least resistance to conserve energy, so filling in an old well might be enough to deter such a creature from coming onto your property. Keep in mind, however, that if an entity really wants to get to you, there's not much you can do to stop it.

DRAWN OR INVITED TO YOUR HOME

Many times someone in the home invites a ghost, spirit, or other form of entity into their house. This may not be on purpose, and you may not even know you've done it, but it happens more often than people realize. Let's explore some of the most common ways a ghost or spirit can be invited into your home.

Séances and Ouija Boards

One of the most common invitations given to a ghost, spirit, or other form of entity is by people, normally kids, dabbling in the paranormal through the use of séances, a Ouija board, or other games some kids play, such as Bloody Mary.

These activities can seem harmless enough, especially if you don't believe in the paranormal or are looking for something scary to do; however, unless you know exactly what you're doing, you can lure an unwanted phantom into your home that can make your life a living hell.

Séances and Ouija boards open doors called *portals*. These portals connect the world of the living to the world of the dead and can allow any type of entity, good or evil, to pass through them at will. Unless you've been trained to do séances or use a Ouija board properly, you shouldn't dabble with these things.

In addition, if you already have some type of entity in your home, you shouldn't use a Ouija board to try to communicate with it, unless, as I stated, you know exactly how to use it safely.

I understand how curiosity about whom or what is in one's home can sometimes make people throw caution to the wind. I've "been there, done that, bought the T-shirt" when it comes to letting curiosity override common sense, and every time it's gotten me into an even worse situation than I was in before.

If you're not trained in how to communicate with the entity in your home, almost any attempt at communication through the use of a séance or Ouija board is the same as opening your front door and welcoming it into your home. In other words, you're giving it permission to be there and, in some cases, making it even more powerful.

One day I was using the Ouija board to see if I could get some help from the other side, specifically from my dad, on a case I was working on at the time.

It took a few minutes, and the pointer answered "yes" when I asked if a spirit was present. I then asked if the spirit was that of my father. It answered, "No."

"Who are you?" I asked.

"A friend," it spelled out.

As I communicated with this spirit, the energy in the room changed. It became heavy, and I was finding it hard to breathe.

I continued on for a period of about fifteen minutes trying to get this entity to identify itself but to no avail. However, the energy in the room became menacing and dark.

"What do you want?" I finally asked.

"I'm going to kill you," it responded.

I recoiled in horror and quickly put the Ouija board away. I then smudged my house twice a day for a period of two weeks in order to ensure that what I'd evoked was totally gone.

Clutter

Believe it or not, a cluttered, unorganized home can attract such spirits as demons and poltergeists. To these types of entities, clutter is chaos, and demons and poltergeists thrive on chaos.

The theory behind this is that the energy in a cluttered home can become heavy, stagnant, and can affect your mood, thus causing negative energy. Clutter and mess can cause us to feel sad or depressed, or even to feel a sense of hopelessness.

These are all negative emotions that can draw a negative entity to your home. Since energy attracts like energy, the negative energy in a cluttered home can attract negative ghosts, spirits, or other types of entities such as demons. The energy in your home needs to flow freely to keep it light and fresh. A messy or cluttered home prevents that from happening.

A clean, orderly house is less likely to attract negative specters and can brighten your mood considerably, thus chasing out any negative energy that could attract a negative ghost, spirit, or demon.

Emotional Upheaval

While we're on the subject of negative moods, the same could be said for any emotional upheaval occurring in your home or business.

In a household that is subject to lots of arguing and other forms of emotional distress, the odds of attracting a negative spirit increases dramatically. As we discussed, these are all negative emotions, and they attract certain types of negative entities such as demons and poltergeists. The same theory applies if someone in your household abuses drugs or alcohol.

Emotional upheaval and/or drug and alcohol abuse weaken us psychologically, physically, and emotionally, making us prime targets for a demon or other type of negative entity to worm their way into our lives.

Negative entities feed off of our weaknesses and, in many cases, can become more powerful. These entities need negative energy, not positive energy, to survive. Remember—bad energy feeds bad energy in the same way positive energy breeds positive energy. In other words, you get back what you put out into the universe.

Haunted Objects

Spirits will sometimes cling to a particular object they loved when they were alive, thereby causing that object to become haunted.

It's possible for an object you buy at a flea market, thrift store, garage sale, or antique store to have a spirit attached to it.

Have you ever been out shopping and wanted to buy something, but got a "bad" feeling from it and didn't buy it? Your sixth sense was probably trying to tell you that there was a ghost, spirit, or other type of entity attached to that object and it wasn't safe for you to purchase.

Most of the time objects that are haunted pose no real threat to the living, despite what we've all seen in movies or on television. However, the ghosts that inhabit these objects can be very active inside your home. So if you're experiencing paranormal activity that wasn't there before, think back to what you may have purchased at an antique store, flea market, or garage sale and see if it correlates to when the paranormal activity began to take place in your home. If it does, simply get rid of the object and the activity should stop. A haunted object is one of the easiest types of problems to solve in the paranormal world.

Ghosts can attach themselves to just about anything, including dolls, stone, wood, furniture, clothing, jewelry, and mirrors—basically anything that is porous and can hold energy.

An object that appears haunted may, in many cases, simply have residual energy attached to it, and while that would be considered a residual haunting because a ghost or spirit isn't really present, it still can be frightening.

Most of the time, the paranormal activity will occur only in the room where the haunted object is kept, although it's entirely possible the activity can appear anywhere throughout the house or business. Ghosts and spirits that are haunting an object can become curious about their new surroundings and roam about freely, as you or I would if we were in a new location and wanted to explore.

I was recently called in to consult on a case that turned out to involve a haunted object. A woman had purchased a bedroom dresser at a garage sale. She was thrilled to have found such a good deal on a dresser that was practically new. She brought it home and proudly displayed the beautiful dresser in her bedroom.

Within a couple of days, unexplained events started to occur in her home—paranormal events that previously hadn't existed since she lived there. Items would be violently thrown from the top of the dresser, and drawers would be opened and clothes strewn haphazardly across the room. This type of violent behavior spread throughout her house in a matter of a few days. Terrified, the woman contacted a paranormal investigation team, who in turn contacted me to assist with the investigation.

A thorough investigation was conducted, but no real evidence showed up on video, in digital pictures, or on tape recordings—yet the activity still persisted. We questioned the woman about any item or items she'd purchased right before the paranormal events began.

She informed us about the dresser and told us exactly where she'd purchased it. We then conducted extensive research and discovered that the dresser had been purchased from a home where a father had flipped out and killed his wife, two children, and then himself—a tragic story to be sure.

Once learning of this, we surmised that because the murders were so violent, the residual energy from the violence had attached itself to the dresser—which was made out of wood—and was manifesting itself in a very negative way. Once the woman got rid of the dresser, all paranormal activity stopped in her home.

It's important to understand that if a spirit was attached to the dresser, getting rid of the dresser would have yielded the same results. Whether a ghost or spirit is attached to an object or if it's residual, it really doesn't matter. In the majority of the cases involving a haunted object, simply getting rid of the object should solve the problem.

Attach Themselves to You

There are ghosts and spirits that will attach themselves to you, making it possible that the house isn't haunted—you are. It's more common for a paranormal investigator to have this happen than a person who doesn't go out looking for ghosts, but it can and does happen.

Sometimes when people die, they become confused and they either don't see the light to cross to the other side or are afraid to enter the light for many reasons—the main one being fear of judgment for acts they committed when they were alive.

There can be many reasons, sometimes known only to the ghost, as to why ghosts attach themselves to certain people; however, certain characteristics in living people can cause a ghost to attach itself to them. The most common is that the ghost is attracted by something in the living person's energy.

If you are experiencing any of the most common signs of spirit attachment—changes in behavior that include increased anger, depression, or suicidal thoughts; sudden, unexplained illnesses; loss of energy; inability to concentrate; headaches, nightmares, panic attacks; or sudden cravings for alcohol, cigarettes, or drugs—then it's possible you have a spirit attached to you.

If you or a loved one is experiencing any of these symptoms, it doesn't mean there is a spirit attached. There is likely to be a non-paranormal explanation for these symptoms, and anyone experiencing them should be completely checked out by a physician. I can't stress enough that a lot of these symptoms are everyday occurrences in many people's lives and that spirit attachments are very rare.

In all honesty, the easiest way to get rid of a spirit attachment is to talk to it and tell it to leave. This lets the spirit know that you are aware of its presence and you aren't going to tolerate it being attached to you.

If you're particularly religious, you can talk to a member of clergy and ask him or her to bless you and your home in an attempt to get the spirit to detach from you or your loved one.

Dependency

A deceased person who was troubled in life, or addicted to drugs and alcohol, might attach themselves to a living person with the same problems. The ghost forms a kind of a kinship with the living person from beyond the grave.

This type of dependency is dangerous to the living person because the ghost, in some cases, may urge the person to continue their destructive behavior, since the ghost doesn't want to lose the attachment and be alone.

The same could be said for ghosts who had emotional problems or a mental illness in life; they could attach themselves to a living person with the same problems or sickness. Again, a dependency forms between the ghost and the living person, which, of course, is unhealthy for the person who is alive because the ghost could be preventing them from getting well or seeking the treatment they require, as the ghost doesn't want to lose its "friend."

If someone you know is addicted to drugs and/or alcohol and you know their behavior when they are abusing these things, you may want to watch carefully for any of the changes in behavior I've outlined.

Many times, people close to a person with a dependent spirit won't be able to recognize the problem, because they assume it's the drugs and/or alcohol talking. Just remember this isn't always the case.

The Need to Feed

Many paranormal researchers believe that ghosts and spirits on the earthly plane need energy, not only to survive but also to interact with the environment.

A ghost or spirit may attach itself to a living person simply to suck the energy out of them over a period of time in order to sustain its own existence.

Just as living people can be energy vampires, ghosts and spirits can do exactly the same thing; however, I personally believe a ghost whose only purpose is to suck the energy out of you is worse, because most of the time you don't realize that's what is happening to you.

It's easy to recognize a living energy vampire because after you've been around them, you feel drained of energy and tired. In addition, most living energy vampires don't realize they are draining people of their energy. In contrast, a ghost or spirit that is an energy vampire is consciously draining you of your energy in order to survive on this plane of existence.

When a ghost or spirit attaches itself to you in order to feed, it is an extremely dangerous situation for your psychological and physical health. What happens is that, over time, the entity attached to you will drain your body of vital energy. This weakens your immune system and could lead to sickness and, in extreme cases, death.

Keep in mind it's not the entity that is intentionally trying to kill you; it's the sickness that can result from your body being drained of energy that can get you in the end. I know, I know, semantics, but there really is a difference. The spirit doesn't mean for its host to die, because then the ghost or spirit has to find another living host, which can be difficult for the spirit to do. The real threat to the living is the increased susceptibility to sickness and disease caused by your body being drained of energy.

The first thing you need to do is visit your doctor to rule out any physical or psychological causes for your symptoms. Anxiety, stress, and/or depression can also lead to the symptoms listed above, along with various physical ailments caused by low Vitamin D or low amounts of other nutrients your body needs to operate at peak efficiency. Various illnesses can cause these symptoms, so it's vital that you rule these out.

If you believe you have a ghost or spirit attached to you, then you can follow the advice in chapter 5. I'd particularly recommend reading the "Rosemary, Sage, and Sea Salt" section of that chapter. A ghost that has attached itself to you, whether it intends to or not, can be considered a negative spirit, and of course the goal is to get it away from you.

The Ghost Moved to Your Home or Business

Ghosts and spirits can be rather adaptable to changing situations and have been known to move from one location to another.

This generally happens when the building, whether it's a home or business, is torn down. When this occurs, ghosts will often simply relocate to another home or business either in close proximity to where they are, or one that is like the place they dwelled in before it was destroyed.

Case in point: Ever since I was a child, I knew there was a ghost named Nathaniel on the second floor of my great-aunt's house. As I've mentioned, the second floor was used only for storage and no one lived up there. Nathaniel was my first encounter with a ghost—my best friend and confidant.

As I got older and learned how to use my gift in a more sophisticated way, I asked Nathaniel how he got to live in my great-aunt's house, as he wasn't related to me and the house had never been owned by anyone but family. As I wrote in chapter 2, he told me that he used to live in an old house on the corner, but it was torn down to make way for a gas station—how vulgar.

Anyway, that's how I learned that ghosts can move from one location to another at will. Since Nathaniel, I've also run into other displaced ghosts and spirits who have moved from one location to another due to their previous abode being destroyed.

If your home or business up until now hasn't had any type of paranormal activity, it's possible that a displaced ghost or spirit has taken up residence and has made itself quite at home.

Came Through a Portal

There are many in the paranormal community who believe that doorways between the world of the living and the dead, called portals, exist and that ghosts, spirits, and other entities are able to pass through these portals as easily as you or I would walk through an open door.

According to some in the paranormal world, portals can be manmade or natural to the earth and can remain open for an indefinite period of time unless someone comes along who knows how to close them—and those people are few and far between.

Portals can be opened on purpose or totally unknowingly by a living person. One of the most common ways a portal gets opened is through the use of a Ouija board or by someone conducting a séance. It's nearly impossible to control what comes through an open portal from the world of the dead to the living, so it's best not to dabble with a Ouija board or séance unless you know exactly what you're doing.

Mirrors

I wanted to put a section on mirrors in this chapter because it's important to know that some paranormal researchers believe that mirrors can act as portals or doors to the world of spirits and that it's possible for ghosts to use the mirrors to visit the world of the living. When this does happen, these ghosts are generally very active.

Now, before you go running around your house getting rid of every mirror you own, keep in mind that while mirrors may be able to act as portals, in most cases something has to draw that spirit through the mirror and into your home.

This means that if someone living in your home is highly emotional, angry, upset, or sad, the likelihood of a ghost being pulled through a mirror increases. This is because some types of ghosts are attracted to negative emotions because they are strong emotions and emit strong energy, thereby attracting ghosts or spirits.

While it does happen, ghosts or spirits coming through mirrors is extremely rare, and in my thirty years of ghost hunting I've only run into two such cases, which I'll share with you now. But remember, I go looking for this stuff; most people don't.

A woman who was highly emotional and high-strung (and that's an understatement) moved into a house and discovered the people who lived there before left an old mirror in a beautiful wooden frame hanging above the fireplace.

This woman left the mirror there, but soon realized that the house she'd just moved into was extremely haunted.

Something unseen tried to push her, her husband, and her children down the basement stairs; items would violently dislodge themselves from wherever they sat and be flung with great force across the room; and doors would fly open by themselves with such force that they almost came off the hinges.

Fearing for their safety, the family soon moved into another house, but not before the woman took the old mirror with her to the new house. The same type of activity started to happen again.

The woman and her husband contacted me, and I could tell they were frightened out of their wits—understandably so. After a lengthy conversation, she finally told me about the mirror. I told them to immediately get the mirror out of their house.

The husband grabbed the mirror, took it outside, broke it into a million pieces, and threw it all away in a dumpster across town. Since then, all paranormal activity in their house has ceased, and I'm happy to report the family is living in peace.

So I know you're thinking to yourself: How many mirrors does Debi have in her house? The answer is ten.

Another such case I worked on involved a ghost trapped in a mirror. It presented me with a very unique challenge, and what appeared to be a simple case turned out to be one of the most intriguing and complicated cases of my career as a ghost hunter.

I was contacted by James, the head of our team, Black River Paranormal. He'd been contacted by a young man named Sam with a rather active spirit who'd taken up residence in his bedroom.

Pictures and posters were being ripped violently off the walls, and various items were being thrown off shelves and hurled across the bedroom. The case sounded rather basic—all signs pointed to a poltergeist.

Sam and his roommate, who wasn't experiencing any paranormal activity, lived in a second-floor apartment of what used to be an antique store. James arranged for us to go out there on a Sunday morning.

The day of the ghost hunt dawned dark and rainy. Thunder rolled through the clouds, and lightning streaked across the sky like a spiderweb as I backed out of my driveway—perfect conditions for a ghost hunt. Sam lived about an hour away, and I had to stop at a Catholic church to refill the container I used for holy water.

Forty-five minutes later I pulled into the driveway of a nondescript two-story building covered in robin's-egg-blue vinyl siding. I met James, and we walked up a claustrophobic stairway to the second floor.

At the top of the stairs we were met by Sam, who showed us around the small apartment. The kitchen was to our left, the living room to our right, and the bedrooms were straight ahead and bordered the living room. Sam's was the first bedroom.

I took my time and walked around the apartment in an attempt to adjust to the energy and see what spirits, if any, were present. The energy felt statically charged and heavy.

Being a typical bachelor pad, clothes were strewn around and laundry was piled up in the laundry room. Various beer cans, half-filled glasses, and empty pizza boxes littered the coffee table in the living room—the remnants of another good party I hadn't been invited to.

James followed me around with the video recorder, and Sam sat on the couch watching me, his big blue eyes filled with the hope that I could extract him from his ghostly situation.

Satisfied there weren't any spirits in the other rooms of the apartment, I turned my attention to Sam's bedroom.

It took my eyes a minute to adjust to the darker room. Heavy curtains hung at the windows and were closed, blocking out what little light was available due to the thunderstorm raging outside.

The large room was lit by one lone lamp that cast eerie shadows around the bedroom. Sam turned on another light, further illuminating the room. The walls were barren, but I could see nail holes and tape marks where the pictures and posters, now on the floor or leaning against the walls, once hung.

A couch sat against the back wall next to the closet; a queen-sized bed rested on the side wall to my right; and a large oval mirror attached to a stand sat in the right corner.

I walked toward the mirror and examined it closely; it looked to be an antique.

"That was the only thing in the apartment when we moved in," Sam offered. "We were told by the landlord not to move the mirror or get rid of it."

"Did your landlord say why?" I asked.

"No. I asked, but he wouldn't answer," Sam sighed, sitting on the edge of his bed. "All he would say is that there was a spirit named Zack in the apartment, but he was harmless. I wasn't thrilled, but the rent was cheap and it's close to my job and my church."

"Interesting," I murmured. "So the thought of living with a ghost didn't scare you?"

"Not really. At the time I thought it would be kind of a novelty," Sam said, blushing slightly. "I never imagined it would turn into such a nightmare."

"So, Zack is the one who pulled the pictures and posters off the wall?" I asked, turning around to look at Sam.

"Yes. See the empty shelves?" Sam said, pointing to three shelves above his bed. "I had my baseball trophies and other stuff on them, but they would keep falling off and hitting me while I was sleeping. At first I thought the shelves weren't level, but they are; I checked. Plus the stuff would fly off of them and land all over the bed. There was force behind them."

"I see," I answered, looking around the room and noticing the trophies standing in the corner.

James sat the video recorder down on top of the dresser by the bedroom door and climbed up on the bed to examine the shelves. He grabbed them and tugged on them, but they didn't budge.

Next he retrieved a baseball from the floor and sat it on the shelves one at a time, but the baseball didn't move an inch.

"The shelves seem level," James said, satisfied with the results of his test.

Taking my time, I examined every corner of the room, pausing now and then to feel the energy, but the room seemed clear—until I got by the mirror. Then the energy changed and became charged with electricity. Something was definitely trying to get my attention; now I just had to figure out who or what it was.

Normally I would just communicate telepathically with a ghost or spirit, but because James was making a video I decided to use a pendulum. I took the rosary from around my neck, kissed the cross, and then let the rosary dangle from my index finger.

"Okay, Zack," I said aloud. "This is how it's going to work: I want you to swing the rosary back and forth for yes and in circles for no. Do you understand?"

The rosary immediately started to swing back and forth rapidly.

"Okay, good," I said. "Zack, my name is Debi and I'm here to help you. Understand?"

Again the rosary swung back and forth quickly. I stopped it with my hand.

"Excellent. Do you mean anyone here any harm?" I asked.

The rosary rotated in a circular motion. Sam and James stood spellbound by the spirit communication taking place.

"Great. Thanks, Zack," I said, again stopping the pendulum from moving. "Are you trapped here?"

The rosary swung back and forth for yes.

"Do you need me to help you go into the light?"

Zack responded by making the rosary swing back and forth quickly.

"Okay, great. Zack, I'm going to move around in the corner of the room by this mirror. When I'm close to you, I want you to make the rosary move toward you. Understand?"

Again, yes.

Holding the rosary in front of me, I slowly moved toward the mirror. When I got about six inches away, the cross jerked violently toward the mirror, repeatedly banging the glass in an excited motion.

James and I exchanged quizzical glances. Why was the cross hitting the mirror?

Perplexed, I backed up and again walked toward the mirror, and the cross dangling from the rosary repeated the same action.

"Zack?" I paused, almost afraid to ask the obvious. "Are you trapped inside the mirror?"

The rosary swung back and forth wildly in excitement.

"Okay, Zack. Hang tight, and I'll get you out of there," I promised. "James, can I talk to you for a minute in the other room?"

James switched off his video camera and followed me into the living room.

"So, what's the plan?" James asked when we were safely out of Sam's earshot.

"I don't know," I shrugged. "I've never had a ghost trapped in a mirror before. I mean I've heard of it in theory, just never ran into one."

"Okay..." James looked at me expectantly.

"I'm going to try to draw him out of the mirror, I guess," I said.

"And what if that doesn't work? What's Plan B?" James asked.

"There isn't a Plan B," I answered, walking away from him and back into Sam's bedroom.

James sighed heavily and followed behind me, pausing only long enough to switch on his video recorder.

Having to focus totally on the task at hand, I decided to forego the rosary to communicate with Zack and have him communicate with me through telepathy. It required less energy for Zack to talk to me telepathically, and he would need all the energy he could get if this was going to be effective.

"Okay, Zack," I said aloud. "This is the deal. You need to communicate with me telepathically—it will help save your energy. I'm going to get you out of that mirror, but you have to promise me one thing."

"What?" I heard Zack say.

"You have to promise me that you will go directly into the light and not hang around here or anywhere else. Okay?" I said.

"I promise. Please help me," Zack pleaded.

"Okay, this is how it's going to work, Zack. I'm going to put my hands on the mirror and force my energy into the mirror. When you feel that energy, I want you to follow it and come out of the mirror through me. Then you must leave my body the second you are free. Agreed?" I knew this was a risky move, but I didn't know any other way to get this poor ghost out of the mirror.

"Agreed. I'm ready," Zack answered.

After taking a deep breath to ground and center myself, I placed the palms of my hands on the mirror, allowing my energy to flow freely from me and into the mirror.

Almost instantly, I felt Zack's energy begin to merge with mine. My hands started to tingle and the feeling swept rapidly up my arms and soon engulfed my entire body. Within just a few seconds, I felt Zack's energy leave my body and felt him standing next to me.

"Do you see the light, Zack?" I asked.

"Yes, I see it. There aren't words to even begin to thank you," he said.

"You're welcome. Go in peace," I said quietly.

"I see my family!" Zack exclaimed. With those words, I felt his energy completely leave the room.

"He's gone into the light," I told James and Sam, who were looking at me expectantly.

"Will he come back?" Sam asked.

"No, he won't come back," I promised. "Now, it's time to clean house."

I walked out of the bedroom and over to my briefcase, which I'd set on the kitchen table. I extracted a smudge stick and my bottle of holy water.

After lighting the smudge stick made of white sage, sweet grass, and frankincense, I walked around the entire apartment making sure the smoke from the smudge stick got into every nook and cranny. As I smudged the area, in a calm but assertive voice I ordered any negative energies or spirits to leave immediately.

Once I finished smudging, I opened the holy water and systematically made my way through the apartment. I kept dipping my index finger into the holy water and making the sign of the cross on every window frame, doorjamb, and door I could find in the apartment.

As I worked I commanded that any type of ghost or entity leave the space in the name of God. I could feel the energy in the rooms begin to lighten and feel less heavy.

"The house is clean. You should have no more trouble," I announced to Sam.

I could see his jaw unclench and the features on his face visibly relax.

"Thank you," Sam said.

"You're welcome. If you have any more trouble, just let James know and we'll come back out," I assured him.

A few minutes later James and I packed up our gear and left Sam's apartment.

It's been a couple of years, and Sam is still reporting that since we were there, all paranormal activity in the apartment has stopped.

This story is one of the most interesting ones of my career as a medium and ghost hunter. It is one of those cases that will stick with me throughout my life—not because it was especially complicated but because to find a spirit trapped in a mirror, to me, is extremely rare.

I knew that mirrors could act as portals between the earthly plane and the other side, but I wasn't aware that a ghost or spirit could become trapped in a mirror.

It wasn't until Zack was already gone that I thought to ask him how he got trapped in the mirror in the first place, but it's too late now. Zack is exactly where he's supposed to be, and I can only imagine his anguish at being trapped in that mirror.

As I made my way home through the pouring rain, I thought about what just transpired. The entire case made perfect sense now—Zack wasn't being destructive or malicious in his behavior toward Sam; he was simply trying desperately to get someone's attention so he could be helped.

This case is a lesson—not just to paranormal investigators, but to everyone. A ghost or spirit acting in what you perceive to be a destructive way could be doing so just because it is the only way that poor soul can cry out in desperation for assistance.

CHAPTER FIVE

PROTECTING YOURSELF BEFORE YOU TRY TO GET RID OF THE GHOST

Before we dive into how to get rid of the ghost or spirit that is occupying your home or business, it's important that you protect yourself against the entity. This is especially important if you feel the ghost or spirit is malicious in any way and likely to retaliate against your efforts to get rid of it.

This chapter is devoted to various ways to protect yourself against ghosts and spirits. Find the one that makes the most sense to you and that you feel you can believe in wholeheartedly, and use it.

LET'S TALK ABOUT FEAR

Your heart beats faster. You start to sweat. Your teeth clench, and your thoughts become numb. You want to run, but your feet feel cemented to the ground. Panic attack? No. It's the average person's body responding to having just witnessed a paranormal event. In other words, your natural "fight or flight" defenses kick into high gear, and you react in fear. Nothing wrong with that—it's only human.

Before we get into protection techniques to use against ghosts, spirits, demons, and other things that go bump in the night, I want to talk to you about fear. Fear is the enemy when you're dealing with ghosts, spirits, and demons. Fear can cloud your judgment and actually make some entities more powerful—not the result you're aiming for. One of the best ways to protect yourself from ghosts, spirits, and other such things is to learn either to have no fear or to show no fear.

Now I'm not telling you *not* to be afraid of demons or malevolent entities; actually you should be terrified of them and seek professional help from a member of clergy or a qualified paranormal investigator immediately, but you still shouldn't show them fear.

What I'm trying to convey to you is that you need to learn how to control your fear, think rationally, and act according to what the situation dictates—not react out of fear and, in some cases, make the situation worse.

The main thing I want you to get out of this book, other than how to get rid of an entity, is to not be afraid of your average ghost, unless of course someone is being physically harmed.

I recently watched a paranormal television show in which a woman was so consumed by fear, and so convinced there was an evil entity in her home, that she refused to accept that there was a logical, non-paranormal explanation for what her family was experiencing.

As it turned out, there was an extremely high electromagnetic field in her home caused by a faulty electrical system. A high electromagnetic field has been known to cause the sickness, hallucinations, and other symptoms the family was experiencing. Once the problem was solved, she still refused to believe there wasn't a malevolent ghost in her home.

The lesson from all this is not to let fear paralyze you to the point where you no longer are behaving rationally and are working yourself up into such an emotional frenzy that you're harming yourself physically, emotionally, and psychologically.

Fear leads to stress, and exposure to prolonged stress can lead to diseases and medical conditions such as angina, asthma, arrhythmia, high blood pressure, headaches, strokes, insomnia, diabetes, and eczema—just to name a few.

There is a time for rest and a time to take action. The fight or flight response is generally short lived, but if what's causing your body to react in this way is not removed from your life, your body doesn't have time to rest, recover, and refresh itself. When the body can no longer maintain its balance, it begins to break down. Illness and even death could be the result.

Why am I telling you this, and what does it have to do with ghosts? I'm telling you the effect fear can have on your body because if you have a ghost in your house, I hope you will think twice about how you react to what could be a harmless paranormal event.

I understand as well as the next person that experiencing paranormal activity can be a scary experience. I've been a paranormal investigator for thirty years, and I still get scared and feel fear. The difference is that I've learned how to control my fear—and I'm going to share my techniques with you right now.

Analyze the Fear

The next time you experience any paranormal activity, stop and think for a second—are you being harmed in any way? Probably not, so why are you afraid?

The answer to that question isn't as complicated as you might think. You're afraid for one of two reasons—you've been programmed to be afraid of ghosts, or you have a fear of the unknown.

Both of these are valid reasons. It's human nature to fear the unknown. The key to overcoming fear in any situation is education. That's why I wrote this book—to educate you about ghosts, their behaviors, their reasons for being here, and how to make them leave.

My philosophy is this: once you know about the phantom sharing your home or business, it takes away some of the fear.

As for me, if I feel fear coming on, I remove myself from the situation for a few minutes, take a couple of deep breaths, and calm myself down. I also use this time to think about what just happened and how I want to handle the situation.

So here's what you do: the next time you experience a paranormal event, stop immediately and first determine if you or anyone else is being harmed in any way. If not, determine how you want to handle the situation—you have choices. You can run, which is a fear reaction; you can say something aloud to the ghost or spirit, acknowledging their presence; or you can simply ignore the event. The choice is yours.

Maintain Control

Remember: the entity is invading your space, not the other way around. You are in control, not it. It's important to understand that you're not always going to be able to avoid fearful situations, so don't focus on what could happen. Instead, control what you can and move on. While you might not be able to control the phantom, you can control how you react to it.

For example, by controlling your thoughts, such as concentrating on the positive and not the negative, you can maintain your calm and therefore your control.

Sometimes I actually bluff my way through this type of situation by saying out loud to the ghost, "I know you're here, and I'm not afraid of you. I'm in control of this situation, not you." I sound a lot braver than I feel at the time, but in actuality, when I do say these words, it helps calm me down and puts me in control of the situation. You can use this same technique to maintain control of yourself and, in some cases, the situation.

Come Up with a Plan

Dealing with a ghost and ultimately getting rid of it is being proactive. You can't be afraid and proactive at the same time. Try it—it's next to impossible. Realize that the best defense against fear is a good offense against what's frightening you.

If you have to leave your house for a couple of days to collect your thoughts and come up with a game plan before you go back home, do it. The end result is that you will be more successful in getting rid of the ghost or spirit in the long run.

When I'm working on a rather difficult paranormal case, I visit the location a couple of times, talk to the people, ask a lot of questions, do the investigation, and then take a few days to think about everything I've learned, do some research on the property, and come up with a plan of action to help the people with their ghost issue.

Taking the time you need to come up with a viable plan can save you a lot of extra work, stress, and frustration in the end. If the first plan doesn't work, have a Plan B ready to execute—even if you don't put it into effect the same day.

Doing this will make you feel in control and empowered so that you can handle the paranormal situation in a calm, assertive manner and therefore have the greatest chance of success.

For example, your plan could be to use this book to identify the type of ghost you think you're dealing with and the type of haunting that is occurring in your home. Once you have that information, you can go to chapter 6 and read through it until you find at least two methods you're comfortable with. At that point, you can gather the necessary tools you'll need to execute your plans. Next, implement the first technique you've chosen, keeping in mind you may have to repeat it more than once over the course of a few days or weeks. If that technique doesn't work, then execute the next technique. You can even alternate techniques until the spirit has left the building.

Have a Support System

Whether it's a family member, close friend, member of clergy, or someone else you trust, talking out what is happening can go a long way in helping to alleviate fear.

Some types of entities, such as demons and other malevolent spirits, try to isolate you in an attempt to gain control. If you have someone you can turn to no matter what, it will make you feel that you are not in this situation alone and that you have help and support.

For example, I have a friend I can talk to about anything, including the ghosts I run across. She's kind of my stopgap to make sure I'm thinking clearly and not going off on a tangent when the answer is right in front of me.

I can't stress enough how important it is to have someone you trust who you can talk to about anything, especially if it concerns the paranormal activity going on in your house or business.

Some people are afraid to tell others about the paranormal activity going on in their home for fear that people will think they're crazy or will look at them differently. First of all, you're not going crazy. Second, if someone you think is your friend treats you differently or doesn't take you seriously when it's obvious you're in distress, then is that person really your friend?

Find the Humor in the Situation

If the ghost or spirit in your home or business isn't harming anyone, then look for the humor in its playful activity. Think of a harmless ghost as a small child with a vivid imagination.

When you laugh, it releases endorphins in your brain that make you feel better. These endorphins can help you calm down, and the fear will dissipate. Truthfully, some ghosts are really a lot of fun and quite delightful. They also can be an almost constant source of amusement. It's all in how you look at the situation.

When I got married, my husband and I moved into a house with at least three ghosts—all harmless. Whenever a certain friend of mine came over and used the bathroom, one of the ghosts would hold the bathroom door shut and not let her out of the bathroom. Our bathroom door didn't have a lock, and she was the only one this ever happened to. Of course my girlfriend would freak out, and I would have to tell the ghost to let her out of the bathroom. I found the situation hilarious—my friend … yeah, not so much.

No one was ever hurt, and the reason the ghost did this to her was because of her reaction; it knew it could get a rise out of her. My other friends also knew about the ghosts and greeted them in a friendly manner whenever they came to visit. The ghosts, knowing they weren't afraid of them, left them alone.

See how not showing fear can actually control a situation and squash some of the paranormal activity? You can employ these same techniques with a harmless ghost with the same result.

Meditation

The goal of meditation is to achieve a state of being in which your mind and body are relaxed and focused. When you're dealing with a paranormal problem, meditation can help you relax, get rid of your fear, and develop a positive outlook.

To meditate, find a position that's comfortable for you; there is no right or wrong position. You can lie down, sit up, or cross your legs—whatever makes you feel the most comfortable. I would also recommend wearing loose and comfortable clothing so your body doesn't feel restricted in any way.

Some people prefer to meditate to quiet music, while others prefer total silence so they can tune in to their environment and body. The choice is yours. You can also light candles or burn incense to help you relax.

Find a place where you won't be disturbed. It could be your bedroom, garden, or a quiet corner of a park. Some people burn lavender, sandalwood, or some other soothing scent of incense or oil to help them calm down. You could also burn a white candle or two to help you relax and give you something to focus on.

Now that you are all set, you need to relax. Start by taking a few deep breaths, and slowly concentrate on relaxing each part of your body. I generally start with my feet and work my way up to my head. This process can take several attempts because we are not used to feeling total relaxation, but don't give up.

Once you've achieved relaxation, take a long, deep breath, and slowly exhale. Do this a few times until you're totally relaxed. Then start to focus on just one thing. It could be anything from the music you may have playing to the flame of a candle to a noise you hear in the distance. Just make sure that what you choose to focus on is constant, meaning the noise or other focus item won't suddenly stop or disappear and break your concentration.

The goal here is to release the fear, so once you've relaxed and calmed down, you can slowly bring yourself back to normal and feel refreshed and in control.

If you're not sure you feel confident enough to try to meditate on your own, there are many guided meditations on audiotapes and on the Internet that will walk you through a meditation from start to finish.

FEAR AND MALEVOLENT ENTITIES

We've talked a lot about harmless ghosts in this chapter, but we need to address malevolent entities such as demons, negative spirits, and ghosts that harm.

When dealing with a negative entity, I can't stress enough how much fear is the enemy in this type of paranormal situation. Negative entities feed off fear and actually become stronger and more powerful. Here's how to handle this type of situation.

Stay in Control

One of the most important things to remember when dealing with a negative energy is to maintain control no matter how scared you are. Showing demons or other forms of malevolent ghosts any type of weakness, especially fear, will make them pounce on that weakness and use it against you. In some cases, they will escalate the activity to keep you in a constant state of fear in order to break you down and gain control. Use the control techniques explained earlier in this chapter.

Dealing with a negative entity, especially a demon or any other type of inhuman, is the highest form of spiritual warfare that exists. You are going to have to not only be very proactive but also maintain strict control of your fear.

It's okay to be scared of these types of entities—anyone would be—but just don't show the entity your fear. Utilize the techniques laid out earlier in this chapter to help you maintain control.

Remove the Bait

Think of a negative entity as a hunter searching for prey. A hunter on the prowl will go for the weakest member of the herd—in this case, the herd is your family.

If you have children who are being terrorized by a malevolent entity, remove them from the home by sending them to stay with friends or relatives until the situation is resolved.

The same thing applies to your pets if they are being harmed or threatened by the entity. Get them out of the situation. In other words—remove the bait.

In some cases, though it's extremely rare, this could be enough to get the negative entity to leave on its own because there's no longer an easy target in the home. This only happens, however, if the adults in the home are strong, show no fear, and maintain control. Even then there's no guarantee, so plan on being in this situation for the long haul.

Get Help

With just about any form of negative entity, you're not just dealing with a run-of-the-mill ghost or spirit; you're at war, and you're going to need an army—even if it's army of one.

Immediately seek out the help of your clergy or a qualified paranormal investigator to assist you with this situation. If you can't find someone to help you the first time, keep trying until you do. There's no way you can handle this type of entity by yourself, nor would I want you to.

However, it's important to realize that you're going to have to participate in getting rid of this type of entity. People can help you, but they can't do it for you.

Be prepared to, with help, reclaim your home, your life, and your family. No one can do this for you. They can be with you; they can tell you how to do it; they can even participate in the banishing of these entities, but you are the key to success.

History, folklore, and various religions have provided us with ways to protect ourselves against unseen entities that invade the world of the living; all we have to do is find the one that we are most comfortable with and execute it. The most important thing about any form of protection against paranormal forces is to believe 100 percent in what you're doing.

Rosemary, Sage, and Sea Salt

One of the best ways to prepare yourself to get rid of a ghost is to cleanse yourself of any negative energy already attached to you. Negative energy can be found just about anywhere, from co-workers to people on the street. Energy attracts like types of energy, so in order to be safe, it's best to cleanse yourself from any negative energy that might be clinging to you and purify yourself.

Rosemary, sage, and sea salt are commonly used to dispel negative energy and cleanse such things as crystals, religious objects, and people.

In order to use this method, you're going to need to purchase some fresh rosemary and sage. Also grab a box of coarse sea salt from your local supermarket. Have a clean jar with a lid, or a plastic container with a lid, to hold the mixture once it's complete.

Remove the leaves from the sage and rosemary and finely chop them. You can use a food processor if you have one to get the fresh herbs into tiny pieces.

Mix the chopped rosemary and sage with the sea salt, and put it into the container you're going to use to store it.

Once you've done this, use about a half-cup of this mixture to scrub your body in the shower or bath.

If you decide to use this mixture, it's important that you continue to use it immediately after cleansing your home, and once a week thereafter for a period of a couple of months. If you run out of the original mixture, you can always make more. This will prevent any negative energies, including negative ghosts or spirits, from reattaching themselves to you.

You can also use this mixture in a bowl of warm water (to melt the sea salt) in order to wash religious objects such as crosses. In this mixture you can also soak overnight any crystals or amulets you have that can't be water-damaged, in order to cleanse them of any negative energy.

Divine White Light

No matter what your religious beliefs are, there is nothing more powerful for protection than asking whatever divine being and/or beings you believe in to send white light to protect and surround you.

You have the power within yourself to encapsulate yourself in the white light as well. In order to do this, close your eyes, take a couple of deep breaths, and allow yourself to relax as much as possible. Then envision a white light coming down from the universe and wrapping you in this white light, kind of like being inside of a bubble.

If you wish, you can say a prayer to God, or whatever power you believe in, while you're calling on the white light to protect you, and include in your prayer a line or two about protecting you against any spirits or negative entities.

The prayer I use is: "My dear God and Goddess, I call upon your love and graciousness and ask that you surround me with your divine white light of protection so that I may face the beings that don't belong on this earthly plane. I ask that you stay close to me while I face these entities and guide me with your wisdom. Please allow your white light of protection to stay strong and protect me throughout this difficult task ahead. Thank you, my dear God and Goddess. Amen."

Please feel free to use this prayer as written or modify it to fit your own personal beliefs. As you say your prayer asking for the protection of the divine white light, remember that it's important that you visualize the light coming down from the universe and surrounding you in it.

Your Mind

Believe it or not, your mind is one of the most powerful weapons you have in your arsenal against ghosts and spirits, and you can use it to protect yourself before trying to get rid of the phantom in your home or place of business.

We have been programmed by many things, such as movies, books, and our environment, to be afraid of ghosts and spirits. Granted, having a paranormal experience can be startling, but you have to stop and think about whether you are really being harmed in any way, other than feeling fear—chances are you're not.

The most effective way to protect yourself against ghosts and spirits is to overcome your fear of them. Most of the time ghosts don't mean to scare us. While you may not be able to control what the ghost does, you can control how you react to it.

There are some ghosts, spirits, and other types of entities—such as poltergeists, demonic beings, avengers, and any other type of negative phantom—that actually feed off of your fear. This is because fear is a negative emotion and causes negative energy to radiate from your body. When this happens, it actually makes that entity more powerful.

By overcoming your fear of the ghost or spirit in your home, you are empowering yourself to deal with the situation in a calm, logical manner, and not enabling the entity to grow stronger and more powerful. This alone may be enough to protect you from most types of entities so that you can attempt to get rid of them.

For specific ways to use your mind to combat fear, consult the first sections of this chapter again.

Prayer to Archangel Michael

If you are a religious person, Archangel Michael can provide you with very strong protection against ghosts and spirits in your home—especially if you feel these spirits may be malevolent.

Archangel Michael is most often depicted as a large angel wielding a mighty sword used to slay a devil. His name means "He who is like God," and he is one of the most powerful angels you can use to protect yourself. Archangel Michael's main purpose is to rid the earth of low-level negative energies and fear.

Simply recite the following prayer—also commonly known as the Prayer to Saint Michael—to Archangel Michael anytime you feel the need to, and especially right before and/or during the house-cleansing process:

> Saint Michael the Archangel, defend us in battle.
> Be our protection against the wickedness and snares of
>   the devil.
> May God rebuke him, we humbly pray;
> and do thou, O Prince of the Heavenly Host—
> by the divine power of God—
> cast into hell, Satan and all the evil spirits,
> who roam throughout the world seeking the ruin of
>   souls. Amen.

AMULETS

No matter what your beliefs are, every form of religion has symbols to represent specific gods, goddesses, angels, and so on. These symbols can play an important part in protecting you before you attempt to rid your home of ghosts or spirits.

The key to using spiritual amulets, as with anything else, is that you first must believe with every fiber of your being that they have the ability to protect you. You must be 100 percent positive that whatever divine power you believe in is capable of putting its energy into the amulet that you've chosen to use to protect yourself.

Before using any amulet to protect yourself, it's always a good idea to say a prayer or a chant, and to ask whatever divine power you believe in to empower the amulet to protect you before, during, and after you attempt to get rid of the phantom in your home or place of business. Make sure you are wearing or holding the amulet you choose before you say the prayer.

The prayer I use is: "My dear God and Goddess, I ask that you infuse this amulet I am holding with your protection, love, and wisdom. Please let the power you put into this amulet protect me and guide me every time I wear it or have it in my possession. Amen."

If you're not particularly religious, you can try wearing an amulet made out of hematite. Hematite is comprised from a form of iron. Some folklore and occult beliefs tell us that hematite has the ability to absorb negative energy. Since ghosts are comprised of energy, hematite could weaken a negative ghost or spirit to the point that it can put up little resistance against your efforts to get rid of it. Keep in mind that hematite only works on negative energy, not positive energy, so if the ghost or spirit in your home is a "good" spirit, hematite might not be as effective.

If you need to go to a store to purchase an amulet, there's a specific way to tell if that particular amulet—be it a cross, rosary, pentagram, or the like—is the right one for you. Have the salesperson lay your choices on a flat surface, like the top of a display counter, then take out your hand, palm down, and place it about an inch above the counter. Slowly move your hand across the amulets. The right amulet for you will just about leap into your hand from the counter—not literally, but you'll feel it's the right one for you the second your hand passes over it.

Another way to tell the right amulet for you is to let your eyes wander over the amulets, not focusing on any particular one. Don't think about which one is right for you, just let yourself feel the right one. After a few seconds, your eyes will instinctively be drawn to one particular amulet, and you'll know that's the perfect one for you!

Now that you have the amulet meant just for you, it's important to cleanse it properly to get rid of anyone's energy that may be attached to it. To do this, soak the amulet in a bowl of warm water and sea salt overnight. You can also use the rosemary, sage, and sea-salt recipe mentioned earlier. The next morning, rinse off the amulet with clean, warm water and dry it with a clean, soft towel. Then set it out in either the moonlight or sunlight for one night or day, respectively, to recharge the amulet with energy from the universe.

Once you've completed this step, hold the amulet and concentrate on what you want the amulet to do—in this case, to protect you from ghosts and spirits. Once this is completed, the amulet is ready to use as outlined earlier in this section.

Some of the most frequently used amulets are:

Ankh

An ankh is an Egyptian cross normally worn as a piece of jewelry, although you can hang one on your wall or in doorways. The ankh means eternal life and is a very powerful symbol in denying evil spirits entry into your home or business. Simply cleanse the ankh after you purchase it as outlined earlier, hold the amulet and put your intention into it, and then charge it in the sunlight or moonlight, whichever you prefer.

Pentagram

To many people, a pentagram stands for evil or Satan. In some circles that's probably true; however, a pentagram is really a symbol for magic or Wicca. Each corner represents something—earth, wind, water, fire, and spirit.

It's believed that evil will stay away because the elements represented by the points on the pentagram are more powerful than evil is.

Personally, I use a rosary to protect myself. Even though I'm not Catholic, I have a strong belief in God, the Goddess, and Jesus, so a rosary works for me. This doesn't mean you have to rush out and get a rosary. You should use whatever amulet personally has the most meaning to you, as it will be the most effective in protecting you.

Again, cleanse the pentagram after you purchase it as outlined earlier, hold the amulet and put your intention into it, and then charge it in the sunlight or moonlight, whichever you prefer.

Cross

The cross is one of the most powerful amulets used by many different cultures and religions around the world—and the one most used for protection.

You can either take your cross to a priest, minister, or reverend and ask them to bless it, or you can used the method outlined earlier to cleanse and charge your cross with positive energy. Either way, the result will be the same—just use the method you're most comfortable with.

When using the cross or any amulet to protect yourself against ghosts, spirits, or other types of entities, don't forget to either wear it or have it in your hand or pocket. The most important thing is that it's somewhere on your person.

CRYSTALS

Crystals have been used for thousands of years to protect people from ghosts and to heal, among many other things.

Some crystals are even thought to be super-charged with protection against ghosts, spirits, and negative entities.

As with any amulet, crystals will need to be cleansed, infused with your intention, and charged in order to work properly.

Some of the most common crystals associated with protection against ghosts are:

Amethyst

The amethyst is thought to ward off negative energy. If you believe the entity in your house is a negative being, you should place an amethyst in every room that has activity. You can also purchase an amethyst necklace and wear it for protection.

In addition, amethyst is a powerful healing stone, and if you place one under your pillow at night, it can help ward off nightmares.

Brown Tiger's Eye

This powerful crystal helps protect from unwanted ghosts. It is normally a brown color with lighter stripes through it when polished.

The tiger's eye is a stone of balance, and if you keep a tiger's eye with you, it can help with gall bladder and digestive issues. If kept in your place of business, it can bring prosperity.

Citrine

This crystal is used for protection and to clear away negative energies. It is a beautiful gold and creamy color when polished.

If you keep citrine on your person, it can aid with digestion, phobias, and depression. It's also a prosperity crystal.

Howlite

Howlite is a creamy white/gray crystal that has black marbling running through it when polished. If you believe you are being haunted, this is one of the most powerful crystals you can use to protect yourself from the phantoms haunting your home or place of business.

Howlite is often placed in the rooms of children who are afraid of the dark in order to help them overcome their fear, and it can be used at work to help with open communication and less confrontation.

Kyanite

This crystal can be one of the most powerful weapons in your arsenal against negative entities. It not only repels negative energy—it literally destroys it!

Kyanite can also be used to help you develop in a healthy manner, and at work it can help you reach your full potential. If you place it by an animal's cage or crate, it will help your pet be free from disturbances and get a healthy night's sleep. Just make sure you place it so your pet can't swallow it!

USING A SPECIAL AMULET
TO PROTECT CHILDREN FROM GHOSTS

Children, by nature, are innocent and haven't been programmed by society, television, movies, and parents to be afraid of ghosts, or that no such things exist. This alone makes them very susceptible to ghostly visitations.

One of the easiest ways to protect your child from a negative ghost, spirit, or other type of entity is to help them make angels.

To do this you will need construction paper or fabric, glue, a magic marker or pen, and any other adornments you want to put on the angels, such as sequins or glitter.

Cut out all the pieces to your angels—you're going to make four angels in total. You will need the heads, bodies, wings, and halos. As you help your child assemble and decorate their angels, talk with your child about all the ways God, or whatever divine power you believe in, works to protect children. This is not magic—it's infusing the angels with divine energy to help protect your child. If you want, you can even put a few dabs of holy water, olive oil, or sea salt on your angels.

Once the angels are completed, help your child hang one angel over the head of their bed, one at the foot of their bed, one on the outside of their bedroom door, and one on the outside of their closet door. Feel free to make as many angels as you wish, and you can hang them on the inside of the closet and bedroom doors as well. The purpose of this exercise is not just to make your child *feel* safe but also to keep your child safe from negative entities.

I've personally used this technique with my grandchildren with great success and recommended it to friends whose children appear to be bothered by spirits at night.

CHAPTER SIX

HOW TO GET RID OF GHOSTS

Across cultures and throughout history, people from all over the world have come up with methods to deal with unwanted ghosts and spirits. Modern-day paranormal investigators and homeowners can employ many different approaches to try to rid a home or other places of ghosts.

As a word of caution, if the ghost or spirit in your home is particularly violent or malevolent in any way, you should seek the assistance of clergy or a paranormal investigator immediately. Do not attempt to get rid of this type of spirit without help. More on this topic will be discussed in chapter 7.

As an individual, there are different ways you can attempt to get rid of an unwanted ghost or spirit. None of these methods is guaranteed to work 100 percent of the time, but they can work in many cases. You don't have to try all of them—that is overkill—but you can employ the method you are most comfortable with first, and if it doesn't work, then go on to another way to remove the ghost from your home or place of business.

The most important thing to remember is that if you don't fully believe in what you're doing to get rid of the ghost, it's not going to work. You have to be confident in yourself and your ability to make the ghost leave. If you attempt any of these methods when you are angry, upset, or frightened, they won't work. You need to be calm and assertive when dealing with a ghost. Assertive does not mean you yell and scream at the ghost; that will defeat your purpose. It means that you act and speak firmly and with conviction. So, let's begin.

TALK TO THE GHOST

As simple as it seems, talking out loud to a ghost is one of the most effective ways to make it leave.

In some cases, ghosts don't realize that they are dead. When a person doesn't realize they're dead, it can confuse and frustrate them, causing them to act out in various ways. Imagine how you would feel if you didn't know you'd died and suddenly all your possessions were gone and strangers were living in your home.

You can try to gently explain to the ghost that it has died and it needs to go into the light. Or you can ask the ghost if it needs help with anything or has a message it needs you to convey to a loved one.

If you're not feeling that brave, understandably so, then you can explain to the ghost that this is your house now and it has to leave. Remember, be firm. Any negative emotions such as anger, fear, or hostility can make some ghosts more powerful, so make sure you are in a calm state when talking to the ghost.

If you've noticed that the paranormal activity caused by the ghost tends to happen in one particular room of your house, or at specific times during the day or night, then you should address the ghost in that room or at that time of day. It will increase the odds of the ghost being present and able to hear what you're saying.

For example, you could say something like, "I know you are here and you may not realize that you're dead and need to go into the light. I'm sorry that you died, but this is our house now and we will take very good care of it and love it just as much as you did when you were alive. It's time for you to leave now. Go into the light, and you will find peace and happiness and be with your loved ones."

Or if you're feeling particularly brave or sympathetic toward the ghost, you could say, "I know you are here, and I would like to help you if possible. Do you have some unfinished business or a message you need me to deliver to one of your loved ones before you leave and go into the light? If so, please let me know in some way, and I will try my best to help you find peace, under the condition that you leave once your purpose for being here is fulfilled."

If you choose to offer to help the ghost and ask what the ghost wants, the ghost could answer in various ways.

One of the most common ways for a ghost to answer you is through telepathy, so clear your mind before you ask if you can assist the ghost. This will allow the ghost to telepathically deliver its message to you. Be aware of any thoughts that pop into your head after offering to help, and if you don't recognize them as being your own thoughts, it could be the ghost telling you what it wants or needs.

Another way the ghost could choose to communicate with you is talking to you directly, so you should turn on a tape recorder in order to catch any EVPs (electronic voice phenomena). Tell the ghost that it can talk to you through the recording device and that the device will not harm it in any way. You can ask the ghost some questions that may help you identify who your spectral visitor is, such as "What is your name?" "Who is the president?" and "Did you need help with something?"

In some cases, although extremely rare, the ghost will try to lead you to somewhere particular in the home where it might have hidden something it values that it wants returned to a loved one. A ghost can do this by "leading" you in a way. It could turn on a series of lights to indicate it wants you to follow it; a ghost could also cause something in the room you're in or another room to move or fall, or make a noise to indicate it wants you to look in an that area.

I have worked on cases in which the people had a friendly ghost and didn't want the ghost to leave, but wanted to set down some ground rules and establish boundaries in order for the living and the dead in the home to be able to cohabitate peacefully.

If you don't mind the ghost being around but wish it would follow specific rules, just talk to it aloud and say something like, "We don't mind you being here, but there are some rules we wish you would follow." Then list the rules you wish the ghost to abide by, such as, "Please don't turn the lights on and off. Please don't bother the children. Please don't turn the water on and off. Please don't walk the hallway at night because you are scaring the children."

If you're going to be inviting the ghost to stay, it's important that you know for certain that you are dealing with a friendly ghost and not some other type of entity, like a negative entity, that is only trying to gain your trust. Inviting a ghost to stay can therefore be risky. It is definitely not for everyone, so don't feel bad if you choose to have the ghost gone rather than having it hang around.

For the most part, ghosts do belong on the other side and not among the world of the living. They will be much happier and at peace on the other side, although they may not realize it. Some people believe that it is cruel not to allow or invite the ghost to go into the light and cross over to the other side. Many of these people feel that in a way, the ghost is being imprisoned and not allowed to leave. The choice of having a ghost leave or stay is up to you and, in some cases, the ghost. However, keep in mind that openly inviting a ghost or spirit to stay may lead to it inviting over some of its friends that are not so nice.

AUTOMATIC WRITING

If you make the decision to help the ghost, you could try automatic writing to communicate with the spirit. To do this you will need a pad of paper and a pen or pencil.

After you've verbally asked the ghost if it needs help in any way, hold the pen over the paper and clear your mind. Tell the ghost that it can use your hand to write down what it wants to tell you.

Most people close their eyes when utilizing automatic writing, but it's up to you in that regard. There are people who have reported feeling very light when they use automatic writing, almost as if they were in that place between sleep and being awake, while others feel nothing unusual but are still successful in their automatic writing attempts.

In some cases you will start writing automatically with no conscious thought about what you're writing. Once the pen stops moving, look at what you've written down.

Automatic writing does not work for everyone, and in some cases the ghost doesn't understand, or isn't capable of doing, what is being requested of it, so don't be discouraged if it doesn't work for you the first time; you can always try again if you so choose.

Don't feel that you have to try automatic writing; it's not for everyone, and it's understandable if you're hesitant to give a ghost that kind of control. Although, keep in mind the ghost is not possessing you in any way during automatic writing; it is simply guiding your hand to write the message it wants you to have.

As with any method of trying to get rid of a ghost, it may not work the first time and can be repeated as many times as necessary. However, after five or six times of talking to the ghost with no results, you may want to try one of the other methods listed below.

The purpose of automatic writing is to open a line of communication between yourself and the ghost. Once you know what the ghost's purpose for being in your home is, you can come up with the best way to coax the ghost to leave. It's also a good time to set down any ground rules you may have, such as not going into your children's rooms.

USE A PENDULUM

A really great way to communicate with spirits is through the use of a pendulum. You can make your own pendulum by either using a necklace that has a chain and a charm that is rather weighty, or you can simply use a string and put something on the string that has some heft to it.

Let the amulet at the end of the chain hang down straight and put the other end over your finger, making sure the chain is perfectly still. Then announce to the ghost or spirit that if it swings the pendulum side to side, that is a "yes" answer, and if the ghost makes the pendulum go in circles, that's a "no " answer.

Start asking yes or no questions such as, "Is there anyone here?" or "Are you a male?" If the ghost answers no to the second question, then obviously you have a female ghost or spirit in your presence.

You can also ask the ghost such things as whether it is trapped where it is, if it once owned the property, or if it needs help.

While personally I normally don't use any tools to help me communicate with spirits, I have used a pendulum when the team is videotaping the encounter so that we can prove the interaction between the living and dead.

The use of a pendulum will give you a better understanding of what the ghost wants and who it is. It will also let you know if you need to find someone to help the ghost cross over to the other side.

BLESS AND/OR CLEANSE THE HOUSE

House blessings and spiritual cleanings are very common whether there's a ghost present or not. If you belong to a house of worship, you can ask a member of clergy to come over to your home and perform a blessing. This normally entails the member of clergy walking through your dwelling saying prayers and asking for God's protection.

If you're not comfortable asking a member of clergy to come to your home to perform a house blessing, you can do it yourself by reading passages out of a Bible. Choose passages that mean something to you to make it more personal.

I use a prayer to cleanse a home or business and to remove evil spirits from the premises. While I'm saying this prayer, I use holy water or olive oil to make the sign of the cross on every doorjamb, including closet doors and window frames. You can also use this prayer while smudging your home or using one of the other methods in this chapter.

The prayer I use is below in its entirety. Feel free to use it or modify it to make it as personal and heartfelt as you see fit.

House Cleaning Prayer

Our Father, I'm sending this prayer because there's negative energy in this house. Please, God, I want a war to start in this home against every bit of negative energy present, including any demons.

God, please destroy every negative entity's connection to this place and stop them from returning by putting a barrier of your divine power between them and all who dwell in this home.

Our Lord, please cleanse this land and consecrate it with your divine power, love, and protection.

Our Father, render any negative energy or entities in this home or on this land powerless, take away all their power,

and have your angels escort any negative energy or evil enti-
ties out of this earthly plane to be dealt with according to
your wishes. Please, God, take control of this home by any
means necessary and protect the family and all who enter
from the negative forces that roam this planet.

In the name of Jesus Christ, I bind every negative spirit
that dwells within these walls or on this land and com-
mand them to flee immediately. I take back this house in
your name, and no evil or negative spirit can enter this
space forevermore.

Our Father, I ask that this home be filled with your
divine presence so that everyone who enters this home or
lives in this dwelling will be blessed with your divine love.

Amen.

Some people might question the use of olive oil instead of holy water, but in reality olive oil is just as effective. It's been used for thousands of years as a sign of God's blessing. In addition, there are references in the Bible to olive oil being used for protection and guidance by pouring it over one's head. In more recent times, many preachers have used olive oil to repel evil spirits.

If you choose to use olive oil, you'll have to bless the oil. This is quite easy, and you can do it yourself. Simply put some oil in a bottle with a cap. Hold the bottle of olive oil in your hands and say a prayer. You can improvise the content of your invocation, or use the text of the following prayer, as suggested by John Mark Ministries: "Most holy God, bless this oil that it might be to us the sweet savor of Christ. May it strengthen us, consecrate us, and preserve us so that we may resist contagion with the sins of the world, and may it fill us with grace so that we may be your dear disciples and faithful witnesses now and forever."

Then put the lid on the bottle and store it in a safe place until you're ready to use it.

There are other ways to bless your own home using incense, candles, crystals, and the like. All of these methods will be discussed in this chapter. Simply choose the method you are most comfortable doing yourself and implement it. Just remember that you may have to repeat this process more than once in an attempt to get rid of the ghost.

If you're uncomfortable asking a member of clergy to come and bless your home, you can take a small object from every room of your house and have a member of clergy bless those objects. Once they are blessed, return the objects to their proper places in each room.

According to many people, this works just as effectively as having a whole house blessing. While I have not personally tried this technique, I see no reason why it couldn't work.

Smudge Your House

The technique of smudging has been used by many Native Americans for centuries to rid a place of unwanted ghosts. It involves the burning of dried sage and sweet grass, or other dried herbs, in every room of your house. Here's how you do it!

You can purchase smudge sticks at New Age stores or online, and they aren't very expensive. You can also use a smudge stick more than once. If you can't find a smudge stick but can find dried sage, that will work as well.

If you're using loose dried herbs, you will need to put them in a fireproof dish before lighting them. If you're using a smudge stick, simply light one end and, once a good flame is going, blow it out. You can use the same procedure for loose dried herbs; light them and blow the flame out, so all you have is smoke.

If you can't find a smudge stick or dried herbs, you can use incense. Try to find sage incense, but if it's not available you can use lavender, rose, or vanilla scents. Simply light the incense and blow out the flame so you have smoke. Then continue with the steps below.

Now, you need to come up with what you want to say while you are smudging. You can say a prayer, or you can say something like, "All the negative energy and spirits must leave this home now. You're not wanted here. This is our home and you don't belong here." Repeat whatever you choose to say over and over again.

Before lighting your herbs or smudge stick, make sure you have access to every room in your house, including the attic and basement. Open one window in a room that is to the west. This will be the last room you do.

Starting in your attic, take the smudge stick and walk around your attic, being very careful to get the smoke in every nook and cranny. If you need to, you can use your hand to fan the smoke where you need it to go.

From the attic, go down to the basement or crawlspace of your home and repeat the above procedure. After you've smudged your attic, do your second floor if you have one or the main floor of your house if you don't have a second story.

Start in the room farthest away from the room with the open window. Start in the farthest point from the door in every room and work your way back to the door of the room, repeating what you want to say and getting the smoke into all of the corners.

Once you walk into the room with the open window, you want to start at the doorway and work your way in a zigzag pattern across the room until the open window is the last place you have to do.

Once you've reached the open window, smudge around the window, say your phrase one more time, and then shut the window.

The reason you are smudging in this way is ghosts like to hide anywhere they can find, especially in attics and basements. So by doing those areas first, you are taking away their hiding places.

The open window is to allow any ghosts or spirits to leave your home in the easiest manner possible. The process of smudging is basically herding any negative ghosts or spirits into the room with the open window so they have no other choice but to go through the window.

You may have to repeat the smudging process more than once in order to rid your home of negative energy and/or ghosts.

Holy Water

Contrary to popular belief, holy water isn't just for Catholics anymore. Anyone who desires to use holy water to get rid of unwanted ghosts simply needs to go to any Catholic church with a clean container and obtain holy water. If you're not comfortable with this, you can use olive oil—it will have basically the same effect.

The Catholic Church has used holy water for centuries in many of their rituals, including house blessings and exorcisms. If you're not comfortable using holy water in an attempt to get rid of your ghost problem, you can request that a priest come to your home to perform a house blessing.

Before you start using the holy water, decide on what you want to say. You can recite a prayer, a Bible verse, or simply tell the ghost to leave in the name of God or whatever supreme power you believe in.

To use holy water in your own house, start at one end of your home and work your way, room by room, to the other end, in much the same way as you would smudge your home. (See the previous section "Smudge Your House.") Remember, you always want to leave a ghost a way out.

You can sprinkle holy water in every room and then put a little bit of the holy water on your finger and make the sign of the cross on the window, windowsill, and doorjambs of each room as you go. Don't forget to do the attic and the basement or crawlspace.

When you reach the last room you need to do, start at the front of the room and work your way toward a window or door on the other side of the room. Apply holy water to the remaining window or door last, so that any ghost who wants to leave has a way out.

Candles

One of the more passive ways to try to get rid of a ghost is to burn a candle in every room for a certain period of time every day until the ghost is gone or until you decide you need a more aggressive way of dealing with the unwanted ghost.

You will need a virgin white candle for every room of your home, excluding the attic (if you have one) or any crawl-spaces. The intent is to get rid of the ghost, not burn down your house. A virgin candle is a candle that has never been lit. You don't want to reuse any candle because, according to some beliefs, once a candle has been lit, the pure energy of the candle itself could be tainted, so make sure you throw the candle away once you've used it and use a fresh, unlit candle every time. You can use any kind of white candle from tealight candles to pillar candles—your choice.

Candles as well as any other porous object tend to absorb the energy around them, so if there is negative energy around the candle, it will become part of the candle once it's lit.

You can either write on a piece of paper your intention to have any ghosts in your house leave and place the paper under the candle, or you can carve your intention into the candles themselves before lighting them.

As you light the candles in each room, you can verbalize your intention to have the ghosts leave. Don't forget to extinguish the candles if you're leaving the house or going to sleep. Also, keep all the lit candles out of the reach of children or pets, and don't put them where they can easily be knocked over. You don't have to burn the whole candle, but you can if you wish.

Remember to use fresh, unlit candles every time you repeat this process. I should add that some people use black candles instead of white candles when doing this because, in some circles, black candles are believed to absorb any negative energy. The choice is yours; use white or black candles based upon what you're most comfortable with.

I've used both black and white candles and normally combine the use of candles with one of the other techniques described in this chapter, such as smudging, a house-clearing prayer, or the burning of incense.

Feng Shui

The Chinese "art of placement" involves changing your living environment to get rid of or minimize negative energy and attract positive energy.

Proponents of feng shui believe that certain things, such as how your furniture is arranged and the decorations in your home, can create negative energy and, in some cases, attract certain types of spirits. They believe that the energy in a space can become stagnant due to a variety of things, including dust, cobwebs, pet hair, piles of dirty clothes, or dirty dishes in a sink. When you clean your home and keep it immaculate, the energy in your home can change from stagnant to a positive air flow, creating harmony.

Followers of feng shui suggest making your bed each morning, keeping household appliances and other systems in good repair, keeping your dresser and kitchen drawers and cupboards organized, and keeping your bathroom door closed at all times with a full-length mirror on the inside of the door. All of these things are claimed to keep negative energy away from your home.

Many people who practice feng shui also believe that your choice of home can make a difference in whether or not your home could attract ghosts and/or spirits.

For example, feng shui experts say to avoid purchasing homes that are located near cemeteries or old battlefields, homes that are dark and damp, and, in some cases, older homes. They suggest that you always ask the realtor if someone died in the home before you purchase it. If someone did die in the home, then feng shui followers suggest weighing your options carefully.

It is also suggested that there are various ways to rid your home of ghosts using feng shui, such as keeping your home clean, reciting the name of God or whatever supreme power you may believe in, displaying objects that are holy to you, or burning frankincense incense or smudging your home.

Personally I'm not a follower of feng shui, but its adherents do bring up some important suggestions about how to rid your home of unwanted ghostly phantoms.

There are certain types of negative spirits, such as demons and some poltergeists, that thrive on chaos and disorder—so much so, that a messy or cluttered house can actually attract such spirits. The same is true if there is disharmony in your life. If your household is filled with a lot of fighting, tension, and/or emotional upheaval, this, as I've mentioned, can also attract some types of negative entities.

Incense

For centuries people of different cultures have used incense to rid their home of unwanted or negative spirits. Used much the same way as a smudging, the idea is to light an incense stick and carry it throughout your home, letting the smoke get into every nook and cranny.

Some people simply light incense in the rooms of their homes with the most activity and let it burn. The most popular incense scents used to get rid of ghosts and spirits are lavender, rose, and vanilla—all very calming and cleansing aromas. If you don't have access to smudge sticks or need a quick fix, then incense is the next best thing.

I'm a big believer in the power of incense to rid a home of unwanted ghostly guests, and I burn incense regularly in my home. Incense has less of the overpowering smell found in smudge sticks and accomplishes the same task.

If you want, you can say a prayer, or in a calm assertive manner tell the ghost to leave while you're burning the incense in a particular room or using it to smudge your house or place of business.

Some of the most common types of incense I use are:

- Mint—Used for protection and getting rid of evil spirits.
- Lilac—To ward off negative energy and evil entities. It's also very soothing.
- Sandalwood—Used to cleanse the home of negative energy. Also used for protection.
- Dragon's blood—Used to cleanse space and ward off evil, among other things.
- Pine—Used to purify the home, banish negative energy, and exorcise evil entities.

If you want, you can burn more than one scent at a time for different purposes—kind of like killing two birds with one stone.

Sea Salt

The use of sea salt to protect oneself and one's home from ghosts dates back thousands of years and exists through a multitude of cultures. It's widely believed that ghosts cannot cross a line of sea salt; however, if you already have a ghost in your house, you're going to want to get rid of it before you use salt. Otherwise you're literally trapping the ghost in your house with no way to leave even if it wanted to.

However, there is a way you can use salt to get rid of a ghost or spirit. Simply get a clean spray bottle and fill it full of tap water or holy water, and add a couple of teaspoons of salt to the water. Shake well and then spray a little salt water in every room of your house. You could even set out bowls of sea salt in rooms that are particularly active with paranormal activity. You may have to repeat this procedure a few times before the ghost is gone.

Once you're sure the ghosts and spirits have left your home or place of business, place a line of sea salt on the outside perimeter of your home or office to keep negative spirits from re-entering your environment.

x x x

As you can tell, there are many ways to get rid of ghosts and spirits. However, none of these methods will work if you don't believe 100 percent in what you're doing. Keep in mind that you may have to repeat one or more of these methods more than once to get rid of your ghostly companion.

Of all the ways to get rid of ghosts and spirits that I've listed, the one I use the most is simply talking to the spirit. You don't have to be a "sensitive," a psychic, or a medium to have success with this method; it can work for just about anyone.

The most important thing to remember is not to speak out of anger, fear, or any other negative emotion; doing so could only make matters worse. No matter how you're attempting to get rid of the ghost or spirit in your home or place of business, it's most important that you're calm and assertive.

USING FOLKLORE AND LEGENDS TO GET RID OF GHOSTS

Almost every culture and religion throughout time has come up with ways they feel are effective in dealing with ghosts and spirits. These methods, handed down from generation to generation, may sound a little offbeat to many of you, but every piece of folklore has a grain of truth to it, so they are worth a try.

Use St. John's Wort

I don't mean the pills; I mean the plant. In the Middle Ages, St. John's wort was used extensively to ward off demons and dark spirits, and it is still used extensively throughout Europe today for that same purpose.

You'll want to put a St. John's wort plant in every room to deter any ghosts, spirits, or demons from entering your home.

Toss Some Rice

An old folk legend says that if you toss some rice on the floor in various rooms of your house, a ghost will feel compelled to stop and count the rice grains. Of course, you'd have to leave a lot of rice on the floors for several days until the ghost, in trying to count all the tiny pieces, gets so frustrated that it leaves.

I know this sounds kind of silly, but people throughout history have reported some measure of success with this method and have also used sand instead of rice.

Play Holy Music

Many people who believe they have a particularly nasty ghost have tried playing holy music every day for several weeks to drive out the unwanted spirit. These people believe that a truly evil entity cannot stand the sound of traditional hymns being played repeatedly, because such hymns praise the glory of God and Jesus Christ. According to people who have tried this method, one should choose very traditional hymns with lots of organ music.

Hang Garlic

Throughout the years and in many cultures even today, people have used garlic to ward off ghosts and other types of dark entities. If you decide to use this method, you should hang a clove of garlic in every room in your house, including the hallways. Some people even carry a clove of garlic in their pockets for extra protection.

While this method could be extremely smelly, it's still quite popular in many sectors of society.

Paint the Doors Red!

There is a belief among certain people that ghosts can't stand the color red and will flee at the sight of it. Such people recommend painting red the door to any room where you may be experiencing paranormal activity, so ghosts can't enter.

There are some people who simply put a red handkerchief or napkin next to their bed at night so they won't be disturbed or scared by ghosts or other entities in the middle of the night while they sleep.

Reverse Your Shoes

A faction of society believes that if you place your shoes at the end of the bed with one facing out and one facing the opposite way, then a ghost will become so confused that it will simply leave in frustration.

Hang a Horseshoe

Sixteenth-century folklore states that if you hang a horseshoe right-side up or upside down above your front door, ghosts or evil spirits will be unable to enter your home. The horseshoe is also supposed to bring good luck to people who pass by your home or enter your home and pass under the horseshoe.

This actually makes some sense if you use an iron horseshoe. It's been believed for centuries by various civilizations that the properties in iron ward off evil spirits. This is because human blood contains iron, and therefore iron would be one of the life forces of Earth.

Use a Mirror

There is an old wives' tale that states that if you place a flat mirror in every room facing the doorway, any ghost trying to enter that room will see its reflection and be scared away.

I'm not sure I would try this technique, due to the theory among paranormal investigators that mirrors can act as a portal to the other side and allow ghosts and other types of phantoms to pass through the mirror from their world into ours at will. However, there are people who swear by this technique, so the choice is yours.

Wind Chimes

The theory behind hanging wind chimes outside your home is that a ghost will be unable to stand the sound of the chimes, and either leave your home or not enter your home at all.

Ba Gua Mirror

The *ba gua mirror* originated in China. According to practitioners of feng shui, hanging a ba gua mirror on your front door will bring harmony and charm any evil entities so they can't enter your home.

Mezuzah

A mezuzah is used in Judaism to prevent evil and destructive entities or energy from entering one's home. The mezuzah is comprised of a rolled piece of parchment housed in a decorative case. You hang a mezuzah on a diagonal on the frame of your front door.

Cinnamon Sticks

Cinnamon sticks tied in a bundle were used by the Egyptians to make an area holy and free from evil. The Chinese also use bundled cinnamon sticks to purify their temples.

Simply tie a few cinnamon sticks in a bundle and hang them over your front door. You can also try hanging a bundle of cinnamon sticks over the doors in your house that open into the rooms with the most paranormal activity.

Gargoyle Statues

Over the years gargoyles have gotten a bad rap and are considered to be evil creatures in some lines of thinking. In reality, that couldn't be further from the truth.

Originally gargoyles served many purposes, one being architectural. During medieval and Gothic times, they were used as rain gutters to drain the water off the roof of the church, although very few still serve this function today.

It's also thought that gargoyles were so grotesquely carved in order to ward off evil spirits and protect the church. The theory behind this is that evil spirits and/or demons were either scared away or they thought the property was already inhabited by evil creatures, so to avoid a turf war, they avoided buildings with a gargoyle.

You can still purchase gargoyle statues today, and you can put one by the doors leading in and out of your house to ward away any evil entity that is thinking about taking up residence there.

Grow Some Rosemary

In ancient Greece, rosemary was burned in temples and shrines to ward off evil spirits and keep illnesses away.

To use rosemary to ward off ghosts and spirits, hang a wreath made of rosemary on your front and back doors, and keep live rosemary plants inside your home in various rooms.

Rosemary is commonly used today by many different cultures and religions. Some paranormal investigators put rosemary in smudge sticks in order to help cleanse a house of negative energy and unwanted ghosts and spirits.

x x x

There are many different methods people have used throughout the years to get rid of unwanted ghosts and spirits. I personally have not tried any of the methods in this section of this chapter, but that doesn't mean they won't work for you, as silly as some of them may seem, so they're worth a try if you choose to use them.

I'd be very curious as to what methods you employed from this chapter and whether you achieved success. Please let me know.

RETALIATION AFTER TRYING TO GET RID OF AN ENTITY

In some cases, a ghost or spirit may become violent or retaliate in a malicious way after you've tried to banish it from your home or place of business. When an entity behaves this way, it doesn't mean you incorrectly performed whatever type of cleansing you chose. It simply means that the method didn't work; the entity is highly agitated about the prospect of leaving; and/or the ghost or spirit isn't going to go away easily.

Some types of spirits, such as poltergeists, avengers, and inhumans, won't be gotten rid of easily and can act out violently at any attempt to get rid of them. For example, a ghost or spirit may react negatively by throwing things, banging on walls or doors, opening and slamming doors, biting, scratching, pushing—or, in other words, doing everything it can to make your life a living hell, and in some cases succeeding nicely.

The first thing to do if the ghost, spirit, or malevolent entity becomes violent is to remove any children or pets from the home immediately. The second thing is to remain calm. I know this sounds almost impossible, but it's imperative that you do so.

Ghosts, spirits, and inhumans are about as unpredictable as they come. Even as a seasoned paranormal investigator, I'm never quite sure how any type of paranormal being is going to react to any attempt to force it out of where it wants to be.

Many ghosts won't leave until their needs and/or wants are met. For example, if you're dealing with an avenger, it won't be satisfied until whatever justice it's looking for is achieved. A messenger ghost may not leave until it's successfully delivered its message, and the ghost of a departed loved one may choose not to leave until it's sure the living people it's left behind are going to be okay without it.

The list of reasons ghosts or spirits could resist any attempt to get rid of them is practically endless; it depends on the agenda of the ghost.

No matter the reason, the fact is that you're dealing with a very stubborn ghost or a malevolent spirit of some kind.

I worked on a case of this nature a few years ago. I was contacted by a woman who had contacted a ghost-hunting team, and they had conducted an investigation. During the investigation, the team recorded several EVPs (electronic voice phenomena). One of the EVPs said, "I'm not going anywhere" and sounded very gruff and menacing.

The ghost-hunting team recommended to the woman that she have the house blessed, which she did less than a week after the investigation. She reported that everything seemed fine—things were back to normal—for about two days; then, in her words, all holy hell broke loose.

Doors would open and then slam shut; the water in the kitchen and bathrooms would be turned on; the family would hear pounding on the walls; and one of their children was awakened out of a sound sleep by a dark shadow looming over his bed. This caused the child to freak out, understandably so, and start screaming until his mother came into the room. By that time, the dark shadow had disappeared. The next morning the terrified mother called me.

Whenever children are involved, to me it lends a sense of urgency to the situation, so I went over to her house that same day.

She reported that before the paranormal group came in and the priest blessed the house, the ghost wasn't that bad. She said it would frequently turn the lights on and off, and she or another member of her family would see a dark shadow out of the corner of their eye, but she notched it up to an optical illusion or a trick of the eye. She also reported that things would disappear and then turn up a few days later in a very obvious spot. The family was actually quite amused by the ghost's antics and called him Fred, after one of the previous owners who had died when he lived in the house.

It became increasingly apparent that Fred was not really ready to leave, if indeed that was the spirit haunting the house, and was quite upset by the family's attempt to make him leave.

After finishing our conversation, I walked through the house, pausing in each room to absorb and analyze the energy. I had my EMF detector and tape recorder running to pick up anything I may have missed and to document the event. Honestly, everything seemed relatively normal, and I wasn't picking up on any spirit activity.

This didn't really surprise me, because it's not unusual for a ghost or spirit to hide if it believes someone is there to make it go away.

I reached the basement of the house—the last place I went, of course. I detected movement in the back corner of the room and quickly headed in that direction. As I got closer to that corner, my EMF detector started to go off and I felt the distinct energy of a male spirit.

"It's okay," I assured the spirit telepathically. "I just want to talk to you."

"I don't want to leave," the spirit answered in a defiant voice.

"I understand that. Let's have a chat, shall we?" I said.

I settled myself on the floor and spent the next hour conversing telepathically with the spirit.

He said his name was indeed Fred, and he used to live in that house. He had a lot of good memories there and didn't want to leave. He also indicated that he knew he was dead but wasn't proud of the some of the choices he'd made in life and was afraid of being judged and sent to hell.

He went on to tell me that he liked the family that was living in his house but was very upset and couldn't understand why they wanted him to leave, as he'd tried to stay out of their way; he wanted them to at least acknowledge his presence. He was sorry he acted out and scared the little boy, but he didn't know what else to do. He was so frustrated with the entire situation, and he missed his wife, who had died two years before he did. This was the piece of information I needed.

I couldn't help but sympathize with his predicament, and I could understand his fear of crossing over. I finally decided that the best course of action was to try to get him to leave by his own accord. It seemed almost cruel to force him to leave.

Gently I explained to him that he no longer belonged in this world, or in this house. That it was time for him to move on, and realizing he was a very religious person, I told him that God was a forgiving soul and that while he may be judged for his actions here on Earth, he would be forgiven in heaven.

Then I pulled out my trump card. I asked him if he would like to see his wife again. His energy spiked, which told me he was excited by that prospect. Finally, after what seemed like an eternity, Fred agreed to leave and go into the light to join his wife and friends who'd passed on. Case closed.

As you can plainly see, there are many reasons ghosts will retaliate after you've tried to get rid of them. While their actions may appear to be violent or menacing, sometimes they just need to know that someone acknowledges them, and wants to know their story and why they are lingering.

I totally understand that not everyone is a medium and can communicate with ghosts the way I do, but there are things you can do to help find out why the ghost won't leave.

Many techniques—such as automatic writing, the use of a pendulum, or simply talking to the ghost—could be just the thing the ghost needs to cross over, and what you need to do to find peace in your own home. All of these techniques are outlined in this book.

If the Ghost Comes Back

It's pretty rare for ghosts or spirits to return to a home once they've been chased out by whatever method.

However, if you were successful in getting rid of the ghost or spirit that occupied your home and it comes back, you can use either the same method you used the first time or you can use a different method if you prefer.

Personally, I think if something worked the first time, then just stick with it and repeat it weekly for about a month and then once a month thereafter for about a year. This can help keep your home free of spirits and let the pesky ghost or spirit that was there before know once and for all that it's not welcome in your home anymore.

There are cases when a ghost or spirit will return after a prolonged period of time. While the reason for doing this is often unclear, if any attempts to communicate with this entity have fallen on deaf ears, then it's time to take more drastic action.

By this I mean: hit the spirit with a few things at once in an attempt to overwhelm it to the point that it will leave again. For example, you could bless the house, light candles, burn incense, and smudge—all within a couple of hours. The point is you want to be relentless in your attempt to get rid of this spirit.

If none of this works, or the ghost or spirit become aggressive or threatening in any way, then you may want to call in a medium or paranormal investigator to help you make this spirit leave once and for all.

CHAPTER SEVEN

WHEN TO CALL IN A MEDIUM OR A PARANORMAL INVESTIGATOR

If you perceive the entity that's invaded your personal space to be malevolent in nature, you feel threatened in some way, or someone in your family is being physically or psychologically harmed in any way, you should call in professional help in the form of a paranormal investigator or medium.

Also, if you've tried to get rid of the unwanted entity that's invaded your home or business with little success, or you're under so much stress because of the paranormal activity that you don't know if you are capable of getting rid of the unwanted entity, then don't hesitate to contact someone who is experienced with the paranormal.

HOW TO SELECT A PARANORMAL INVESTIGATOR AND/OR MEDIUM

Thousands of paranormal investigators and ghost-hunting teams are out there, and it can be difficult to know which one to choose to assist you in getting rid of your unwanted and uninvited houseguest. However, you can take certain steps to ensure you get the right paranormal investigator or ghost-hunting team for you.

First Contact

Very few paranormal investigators and ghost-hunting teams list their telephone number on their websites, and who can blame them? They don't want to get prank calls at all hours of the day and night. However, there should be an email address or online form you can fill out requesting help, and I would recommend you do so.

One of the members of the ghost-hunting team should contact you to find out more about your situation. Most ghost-hunting teams have one of their members contact those who email the team or submit an online request.

I know of one extreme group that doesn't contact anyone by phone but sends those who inquire a package filled with lengthy forms and questions that need to be filled out and returned. This group has been known to turn down cases because there's too much activity, or because they feel the activity is being caused by a negative entity, and/or there isn't enough activity to warrant them wasting their time. I know, hard to believe.

You want to avoid any ghost-hunting team that makes you jump through hoops before they will telephone you, gives you a list of criteria that must be met, or tells you that you have activity they aren't interested in investigating.

You also want to avoid any paranormal investigator or ghost-hunting team that wants to charge you right away. Most reputable investigators won't charge you to investigate your home; however, some may charge for traveling expenses if they reside out of your state or a long distance away. This should not deter you from hiring such a team, as such expenses are well within reason.

I recommend that you keep contacting paranormal investigators until you find one that contacts you back and is genuinely interested in helping you with your problem.

Interview the Paranormal Investigator, Ghost Hunter, or Medium

Come up with some questions you want to ask any ghost hunter or paranormal investigator who contacts you. Remember, you're hiring them, and of course you have the right to interview any prospective person you plan on inviting into your home or business. You will also want to avoid any paranormal team that doesn't do a follow-up after the investigation and offer to help you with your problem ghost.

Following is a list of questions you may want to ask:

- How long have you been a paranormal investigator/ ghost hunter?

- What kind of equipment do you use?
- How many people would you be bringing with you, and what is their experience?
- Have you or any member of your team ever been arrested? If so, for what?
- Have you or any member of your team been convicted of a crime? What crime?
- Do you or any member of your team use drugs?
- Does any member of your team drink excessive amounts of alcohol?
- Does any member of your team have any psychological disorders? If so, what?
- Have you and/or your team ever dealt with a situation like mine?
- If so, what was the outcome and how was that achieved?
- Do you give a full report after you've analyzed all the evidence you collect in my house?
- What time would you arrive at my house and how long will the investigation take?
- Do you have references I can contact?
- Do you have a phone number where I can reach you in case of an emergency or if I need to reschedule?

This is just a small sampling of the questions to which you may want answers. Feel free to add your own questions that relate to your individual situation.

Ask for References

Any ghost-hunting team or paranormal investigator who is worth your time should be able to provide you with a list of references you can communicate with.

Before you contact the references, come up with a list of questions you want answered. You will want to know if the investigator was professional, respectful, on time, appeared to be competent, and gave a full report of their findings—just to name a few items. Don't hesitate to contact all or as many of the references as you want.

Listen carefully to how the references answer the questions, and ask follow-up questions if necessary. Ask them if they would use that paranormal investigator again and if they would recommend them to friends, family, and co-workers.

Final Selection

Once you've interviewed several paranormal investigators and / or ghost-hunting teams and contacted their references, it's time for you to make a decision as to whether or not you want to hire one of those teams or keep looking.

Assuming you're satisfied with the references and answers to the interview questions you've asked, choose the team that you feel most comfortable with. Don't ever forget that you are inviting these people into your home, so it's important that you are satisfied with your decision. Also remember that you have the right to make them stop the investigation at any time and to ask them to leave if you feel their behavior isn't professional or if it makes you uncomfortable in any way.

WHAT TO EXPECT DURING A PARANORMAL INVESTIGATION

Paranormal investigations are very invasive—not only physically but personally as well. A good paranormal investigator is going to ask a lot of questions—many of them personal, such as whether anyone in the household is on drugs, including prescription drugs, and what they are for; whether anyone in the house suffers from clinically diagnosed depression; or whether anyone drinks alcohol and how much. They may also ask about the personal relationships between people living in the house, or how co-workers get along if it's a place of business.

They are not asking these questions out of idle curiosity. The answers to these questions are important because they give the investigator answers as to how the paranormal activity is being perceived by people who live in the house or work in the business.

A lot of different people will be coming in and out of your home or business, setting up all kinds of different equipment. The equipment could include video cameras, wireless DVR cameras, tape recorders, electromagnetic detectors, and so on. There could be wires stretching from one end of your house to the other. All of this is necessary so that the investigators can gather as much information as possible in order to come to an accurate conclusion about what is going on.

If you have children and/or pets, arrange to have them out of the house when the investigation takes place. You don't want to unduly scare your children, and pets can get overly excited and interfere with the investigation. In addition, if an entity gets angry that you've called in a paranormal investigation team, it could retaliate by injuring one of your children or pets. The goal is to keep everyone and everything safe.

When our team shows up for an investigation, the first thing we do after we bring in all the equipment is a walk-through of the house or place of business with the owners, so they can tell us what they've experienced and where.

Then our tech department sets up the wireless DVR cameras in the appropriate locations based on what the homeowner has told us.

Once we're ready to get started, we all gather outside in a circle and say a prayer of protection. Then we divide into teams and grab our other equipment, such as digital cameras, tape recorders, video cameras, EVP detectors, and anything else we may need.

Then the teams go their own ways and to opposite sides of the house to keep from contaminating any evidence the other team might pick up.

We continue to rotate teams and locations within the building for several hours and sometimes well into the early-morning hours before we pack up our equipment and head out into the night to analyze our findings.

AFTER THE INVESTIGATION

Once an investigation is concluded, the team you hire will pack up their equipment and take a few days to analyze all the recordings and the like and come to a conclusion about what is going on in your home or business.

A primary member of the team should meet with you after this is completed to go over the results and suggest a course of action, such as a house blessing or cleaning. This person should be able to help you find someone who is trained to do such a blessing or cleaning if a member of their team doesn't perform these services.

If you're not satisfied for any reason with what the paranormal team you hired tells you, or if they don't have a viable plan to help you get rid of the entity, then don't hesitate to contact another paranormal team to help you.

Remember: the goal is to bring the entire situation to a satisfactory conclusion for you and the ghost or spirit.

THE USE OF A MEDIUM

Having a medium come to your home is a little bit different from having a team of paranormal investigators come into your home. For one thing, a medium generally works alone or with one other person.

While a medium may bring a tape recorder and/or a camera, a medium going through your home is much less invasive than a group of paranormal investigators.

Generally, mediums will be very quiet and not cause a lot of commotion but will walk through the house and explore every room until they locate the ghost or spirit.

Just as you would if you were hiring a paranormal investigator, you're going to want to interview more than one medium until you find one you feel comfortable with and who seems to genuinely care about what you and your family are experiencing and wants to help.

Don't be afraid of offending a medium by asking for references; and if the medium acts insulted or delays providing them to you, then that's not the right medium for you.

One last word of advice when you're considering hiring a medium: every medium works differently and has unique methods for communicating with ghosts, spirits, or other types of entities that may be lurking in your home. Some of these methods might seem a little strange but don't hold that against the medium.

It's important to remember that most mediums generally walk a very thin line between the world of the living and the world of the dead. They have to do whatever it takes to maintain balance between these two worlds, and sometimes the techniques they use to accomplish that goal could seem a little bizarre to the typical person. So it's important for you to accept how the medium you hire to help you deals with both worlds, and remember the medium is there to help you.

When I arrive at a location as a medium, I spend a lot of time talking to the homeowners about their experiences, their fears, their concerns, and what their goals are—i.e., whether they just want to know who the ghost is and why it is there, or whether they want the ghost, spirit, or other type of entity gone.

Then I walk through the house room by room, touching walls, furniture, or any other object that I'm drawn to, so that I can read the energy from those items. I continue going through the house in this methodical fashion until I encounter the entity, if there is one, and then I try to engage it in conversation.

While all this is going on, the homeowners are generally hot on my heels, which is good because they are readily available should I have any questions.

Once I've established communication, I try to negotiate with the entity to get it to go into the light or leave by whatever method it chooses. Once the spirit has left, or I have forced it out, I do a house blessing and smudging to clear out any residual negative energy.

Having a medium come into your home is a lot less invasive than a team of paranormal investigators. I try to keep the process very calm and peaceful to help relax the homeowners and any entity that may be present.

CHAPTER EIGHT

HOW TO KEEP YOUR SPACE SPIRIT-FREE

Once the ghost, spirit, or whatever other type of phantom has left your home or place of business, in all probability, you're going to want to keep it gone. There are various methods you can use for this purpose, and they are directly related to how you got rid of the specter originally—same method, slightly different purpose.

SEA SALT

Once any type of ghost is out of your house, you're going to want to purchase several boxes of sea salt. It's widely believed by many paranormal investigators and others that a negative entity cannot cross a line of salt.

Take the sea salt and sprinkle it around the perimeter of the outside of your home. You're going to want to repeat this procedure about once a month, as the salt will be washed away by rain and blown away by the wind. If you live in an apartment, you can take the sea salt and place a small bowl of it in each room to absorb any negative energies that attempt to come into your personal space. Make sure to change the salt in the bowls once a week.

HOLY WATER OR OLIVE OIL

If you decide to use holy water or olive oil that you've blessed according to the ritual in chapter 5, you are going to want to keep a supply on hand.

About once a month you're going to use the holy water and/or olive oil to make the sign of the cross on every door, including inside doors and on the glass of every window. Don't forget to say a prayer of blessing, such as the Prayer to Saint Michael the Archangel, when you are performing this ritual. The prayer will give what you are doing more positive energy and help to strengthen the power of the holy water or olive oil.

SMUDGING

After the ghost, spirit, or other type of phantom is gone, you want to keep the energy in your home positive, especially if you have just expelled negative energy in the form of a malevolent phantom.

Smudging is one of the quickest, easiest, and most effective ways to keep your home or place of business free of negative energy. Instructions for smudging are in chapter 6, so refer back to that chapter if need be.

You should smudge your home once a week for a month after it is ghost-free, and then once every other week for another month, and then once a month thereafter for six months to a year. You can smudge longer if you wish; the choice is entirely yours.

CANDLES

I don't know about you, but personally I love candles. Not just to get rid of ghosts or other types of unwanted guests, but I find them relaxing, and they create a wonderful atmosphere in any room.

You can burn candles anytime, whether or not you used the candle method to get rid of the spirits in your home or business. However, if you're using candles strictly to keep ghosts out, then I would recommend burning a white virgin (never-been-lit) candle in every room of your home at least once a week for three or four months after the unwanted ghost is gone.

You can burn them more frequently if you wish, but remember: never leave a candle unattended, and always keep candles out of the reach of children and pets. The goal is to keep the ghost away, not burn down your house.

INCENSE

If you want to use incense to keep unwanted spirits away, you can follow the same directions as for candles. Burn incense pretty much anytime you want; but to make sure the ghost that just left doesn't return, you can burn incense at least once a week for three to six months.

I recommend the incense listed in chapter 6, as those particular scents have proved effective in keeping away ghosts, spirits, and some other types of entities.

Sandalwood incense is my personal favorite—not only because I like the aroma, but also because it can assist in keeping ghosts away and works to help protect you from negative energies.

CRYSTALS

Crystals are very interesting and powerful items to have. Many people believe they are capable of doing amazing things, not only in your fight against ghosts but also in other aspects of your life.

If you're going to use crystals to keep your home ghost-free, use the types of crystals mentioned in chapter 5. You can leave crystals sitting out in every room of your home. You can carry them on you in the form of jewelry or just in your pocket. Or you can do both.

Since crystals require very little maintenance, I suggest leaving them in every room of your home indefinitely. Or if you choose not to do that, you should leave crystals in every room of your home for at least six months after getting rid of the ghost, spirit, or other phantom that haunted your personal space.

Don't forget that at least once a month you will need to cleanse and recharge your crystals by letting them soak in salt water overnight, and then hold them and fill them with your intent, such as protection from ghosts. Finally, set your crystals out in the sunlight all day or the moonlight all night.

FINAL THOUGHTS

I sincerely hope you found this book to be helpful and meaningful. I greatly enjoyed writing it to share with all of you—my readers.

It is my sincere desire that you now have a better understanding of ghosts and the world of the paranormal, and that you've had great success in handling your ghost issue.

I believe that many harmless ghosts and spirits are some of the most misunderstood beings in our world. It's been my experience that most ghosts are just trying to eke out their existence like we are—albeit from a totally different perspective. Yet the fact remains that in the vast majority of cases, if not all of them, ghosts and spirits no longer should be in the world of the living, but rather should make the transition to the freedom and peace of crossing over to the other side.

Throughout my life I've come in contact with hundreds, if not thousands, of ghosts and spirits—some good, some bad, just like the living. I've become good friends with some of the phantoms that have drifted in and out of my life, and I've shared countless hours conversing with them on many topics. In general, I'm much more comfortable among the dead than the living.

But the time always comes when I have to say goodbye, as I help them make the transition from our world into theirs—on the other side of the veil that separates the two. I've had my heart broken when I have to see them go, yet I know it's where they belong and it's for the best.

The most important thing I want you to take away from this book is that you have the power within yourself to handle most paranormal experiences that arise.

Know also that while all of the methods outlined in this book can work, they will only be effective if you use them without being in a state of fear and if you believe 100 percent in what you're doing—anything less, and there's no technique for getting rid of a ghost in this world that will work for you.

It all boils down to faith. You have to have faith in yourself, whatever divine power you believe in, and total trust in any people you choose to assist you with your ghost or spirit.

It's my sincere desire that you step into your own power and not allow yourself to be crippled in fear of the unknown or the paranormal. Don't be afraid to claim your personal space and let any type of entity in your home know that you are not afraid, that you won't tolerate it being in your space, and that you will be proactive in getting the ghost, spirit, or other type of entity to leave you and your family alone.

Don't hesitate to ask for help if you feel you can't handle the ghost, spirit, or other type of entity in your home or business. As I've stated, there are some types of paranormal entities that you shouldn't mess with no matter how brave you feel. There's no shame in asking for help, especially when dealing with a negative, malevolent, or demonic entity—it may be your only chance.

Your main goal, and mine, is that no matter what type of entity has invaded your personal space, it is imperative that you keep yourself and your family safe—even if that means a period of separation until you can get the paranormal situation under control or resolved.

I have one golden rule that guides my life when it comes to the paranormal: if you don't know what it is, don't mess with it until you do.

As I've outlined in this book, different types of entities behave in different ways and are capable of doing many things—some of them harmful to the living. Therefore, until you can identify what type of specter you're dealing with, leave it alone. If you're feeling you have lost control of the situation or are unable to handle the paranormal activity on your own, don't hesitate to contact a paranormal investigator, a medium, or a member of clergy to help you.

Only when you're pretty certain what type of entity is involved and have a solid plan of attack should you spring into action and attempt to get that entity to vacate the premises.

It's also important to remember that, just like the living, no two ghosts are exactly alike, and they all have their own unique personalities. Some ghosts or spirits may exhibit characteristics of more than one type of specific ghost. At times, this can make it rather confusing as to what type of ghost you have in your home or business. When this happens, do what I do—make your best guess and act accordingly.

My own personal philosophy is that in the case of a harmless ghost, the best solution for everybody is to try to assist the ghost in fulfilling whatever reason it has for lingering in the earthly plane.

The most effective way of doing this is simply to talk to the spirit or try one of the techniques outlined in this book to communicate with it—never losing sight of the goal, which is to help the ghost get to the other side in the most effective way possible.

I call it *spirit rescue*. I believe that helping the entity also helps the people who are being affected by the ghost or spirit. It's a win-win situation for everybody involved. Trust me when I say that there isn't much that is more rewarding than helping a ghost or spirit cross over and helping it find peace. If you're still unsure about helping a spirit, that's okay—find someone who will do it for you. The real question you have to ask yourself is this: if you were that spirit, wouldn't you want someone to help you?

I hope that this book is helpful—not just for homeowners or business owners but for everyone, including paranormal investigators. While it may appear that a ghost or spirit is acting out in a destructive or aggressive manner, it could be the only way some poor soul can cry out in desperation for assistance.

In closing, I want you to know that, as always, I'm right there with you. Don't hesitate to contact me if you have questions or need help with your paranormal situation. There's no reason to feel any shame in admitting you have a ghost problem; and while some people might judge you and think you're nuts, you're not. You just need help with a very extraordinary situation. You can email me at debichestnut @yahoo.com. I do answer all my emails and will try my very best to help you with your paranormal questions and issues.

Until the next book ... Happy Hauntings!

To Write to the Author

If you wish to contact the author or would like more information about this book, please write to the author in care of Llewellyn Worldwide Ltd. and we will forward your request. Both the author and the publisher appreciate hearing from you and learning of your enjoyment of this book and how it has helped you. Llewellyn Worldwide Ltd. cannot guarantee that every letter written to the author can be answered, but all will be forwarded. Please write to:

Debi Chestnut
⁄ Llewellyn Worldwide
2143 Wooddale Drive
Woodbury, MN 55125-2989

Please enclose a self-addressed stamped envelope for reply, or $1.00 to cover costs. If outside the USA, enclose an international postal reply coupon.